Leaves of Peace
Coloring Book
Relaxation & Stress Relieving Patterns

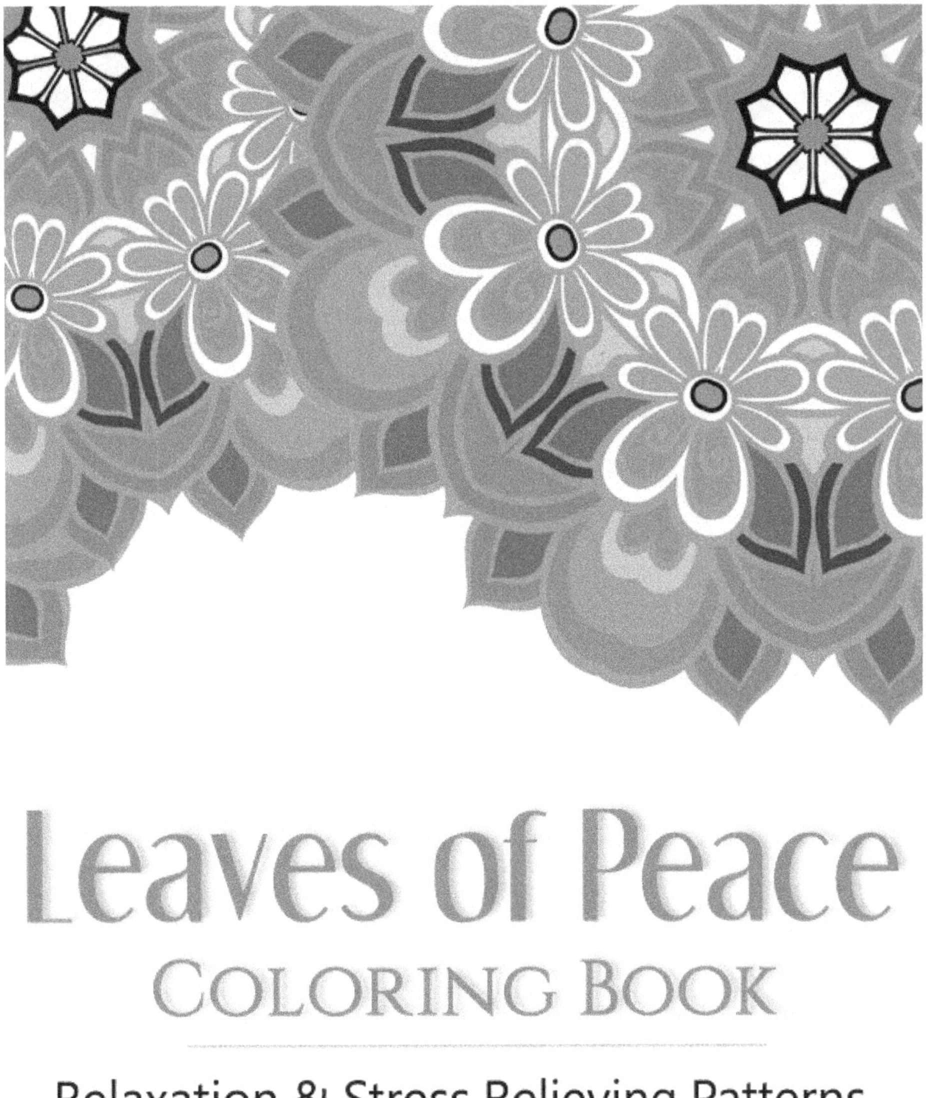

Vol. 24

V ART™

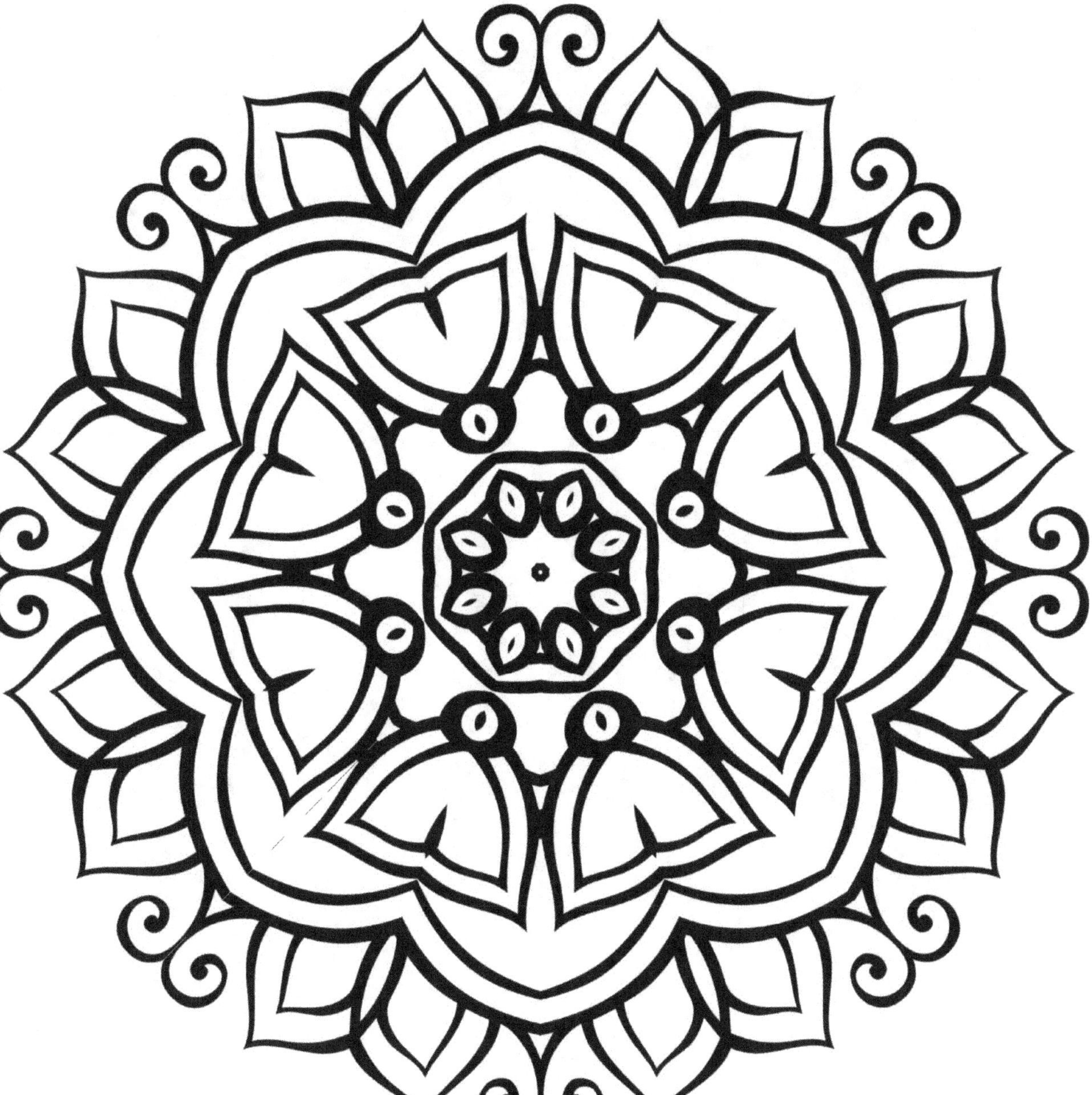

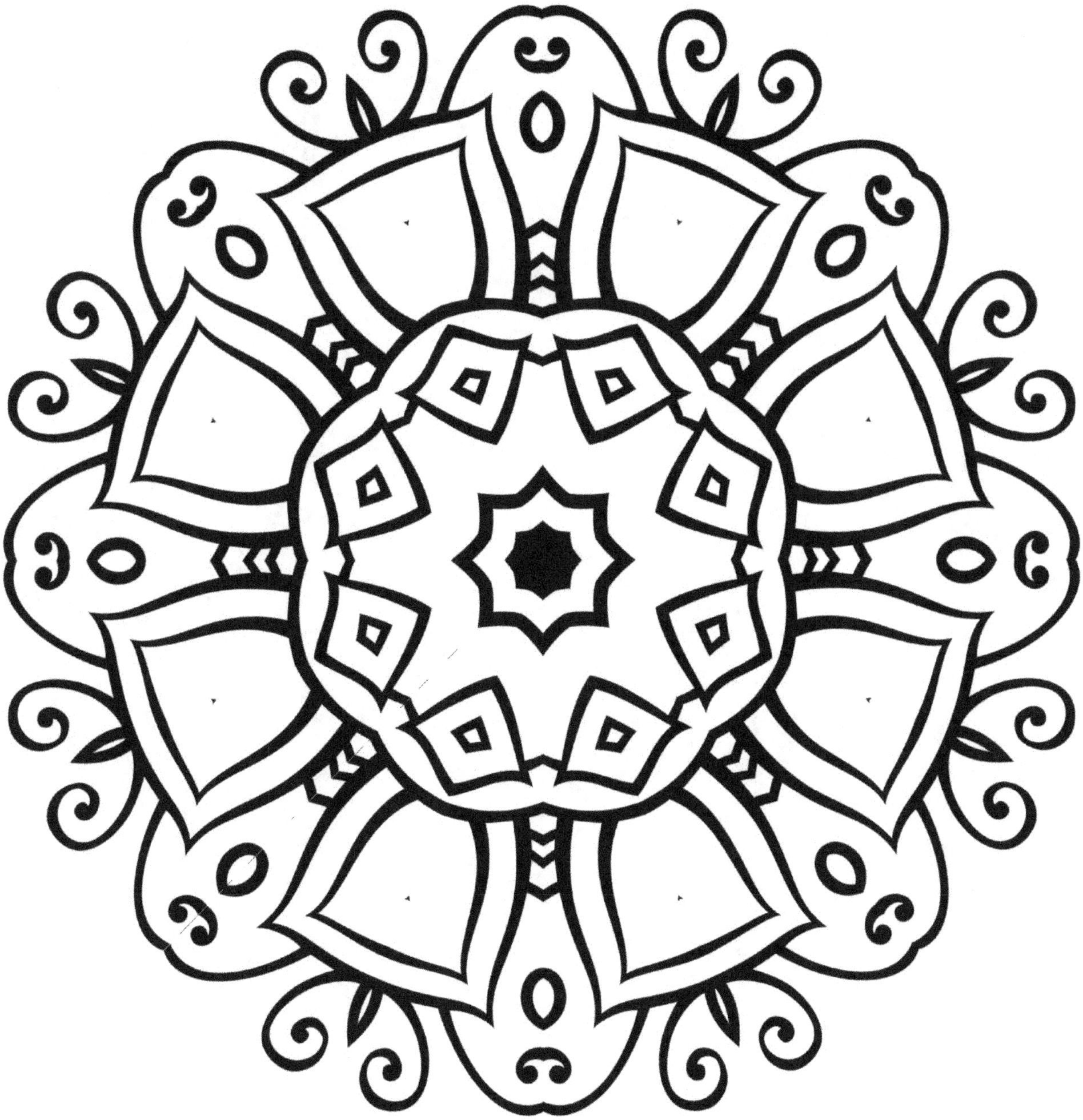

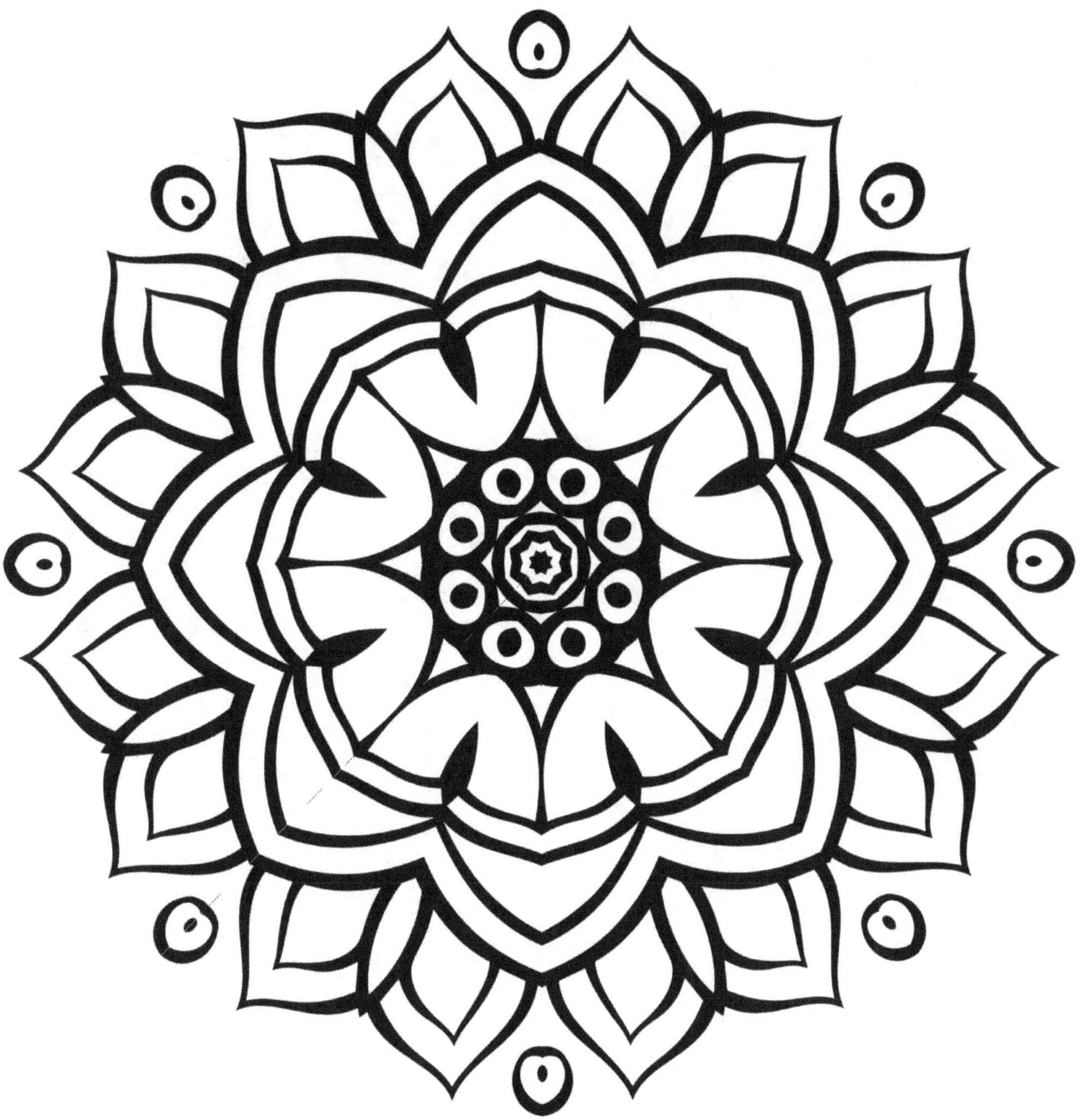

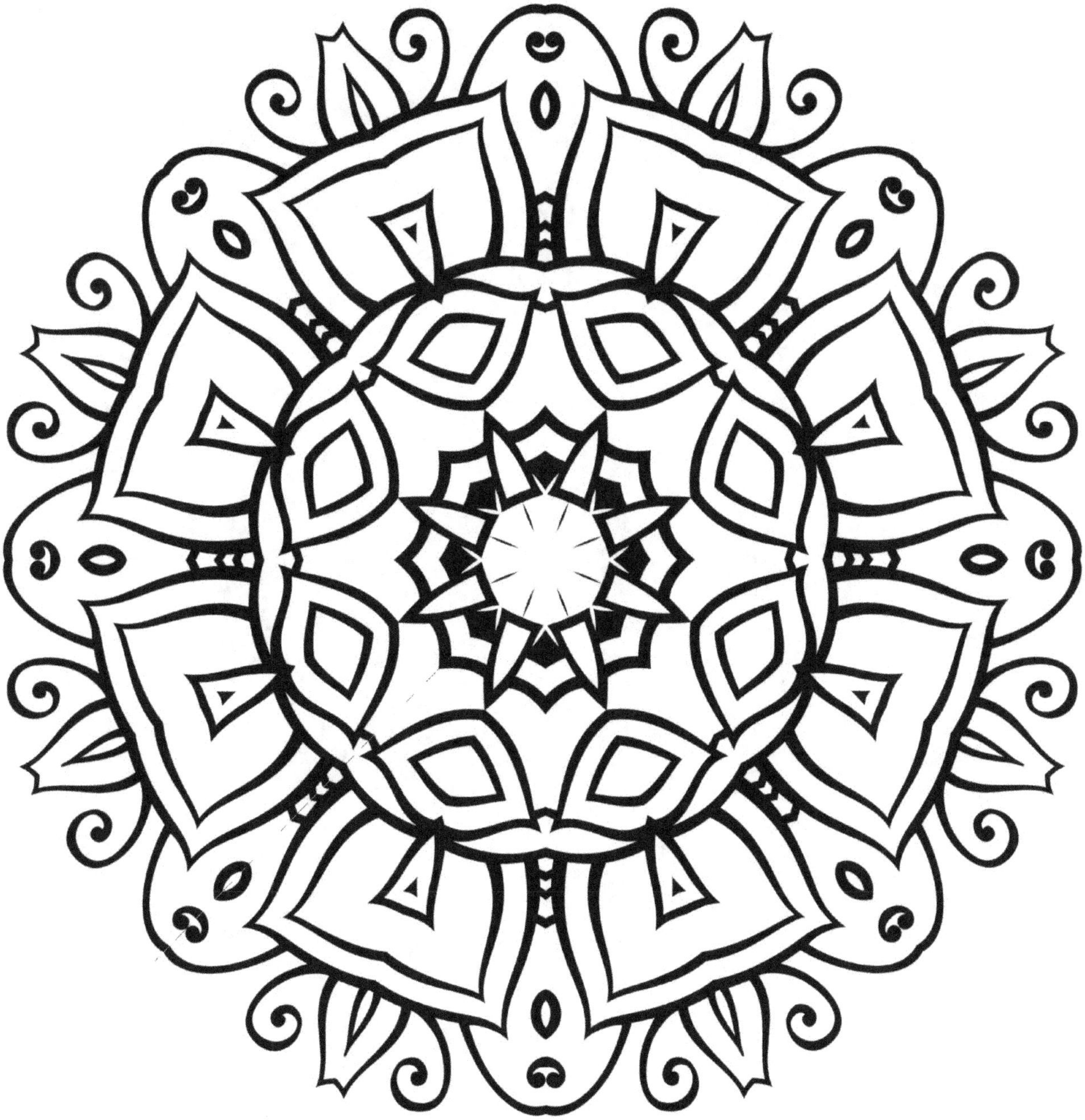

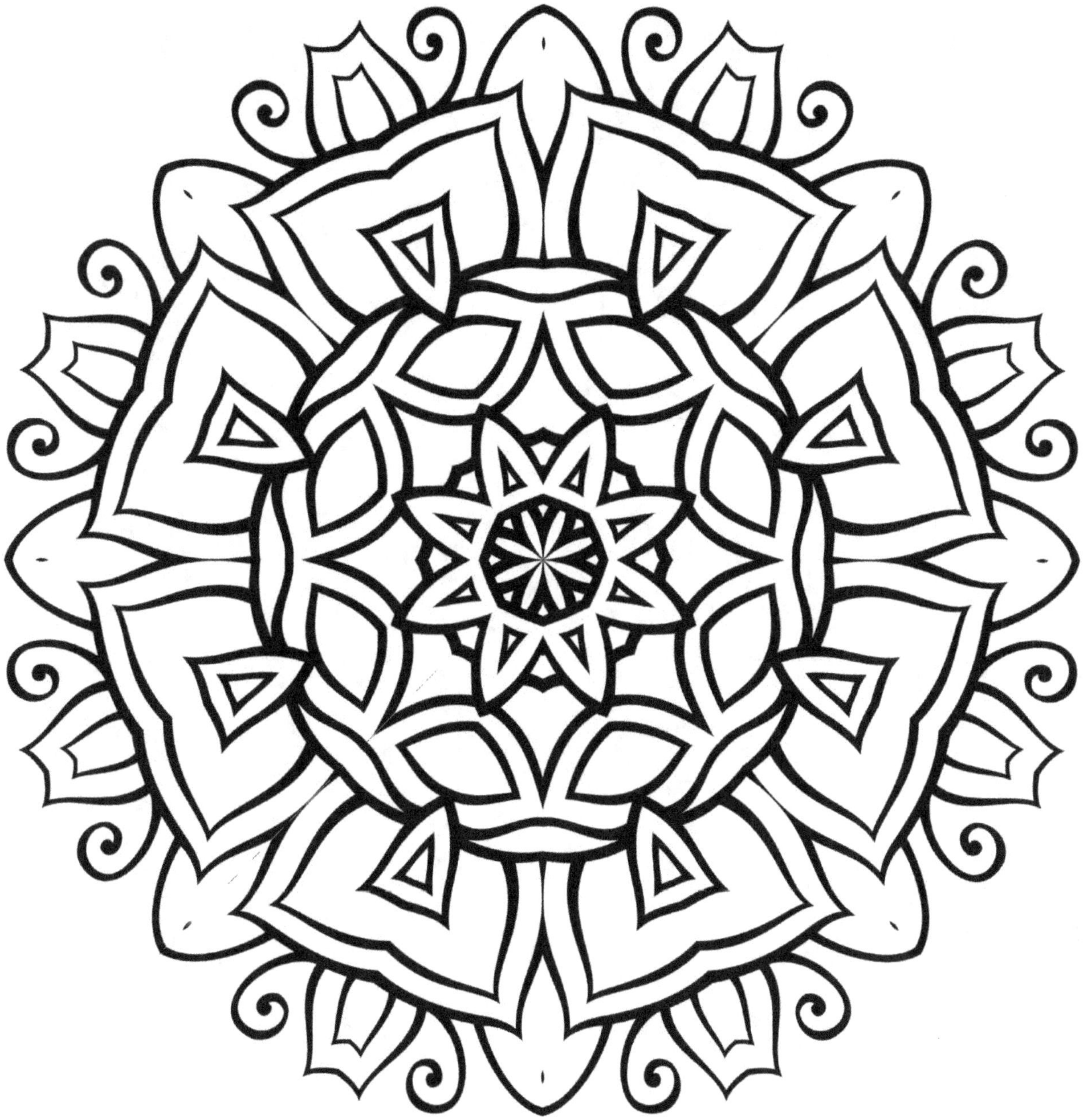

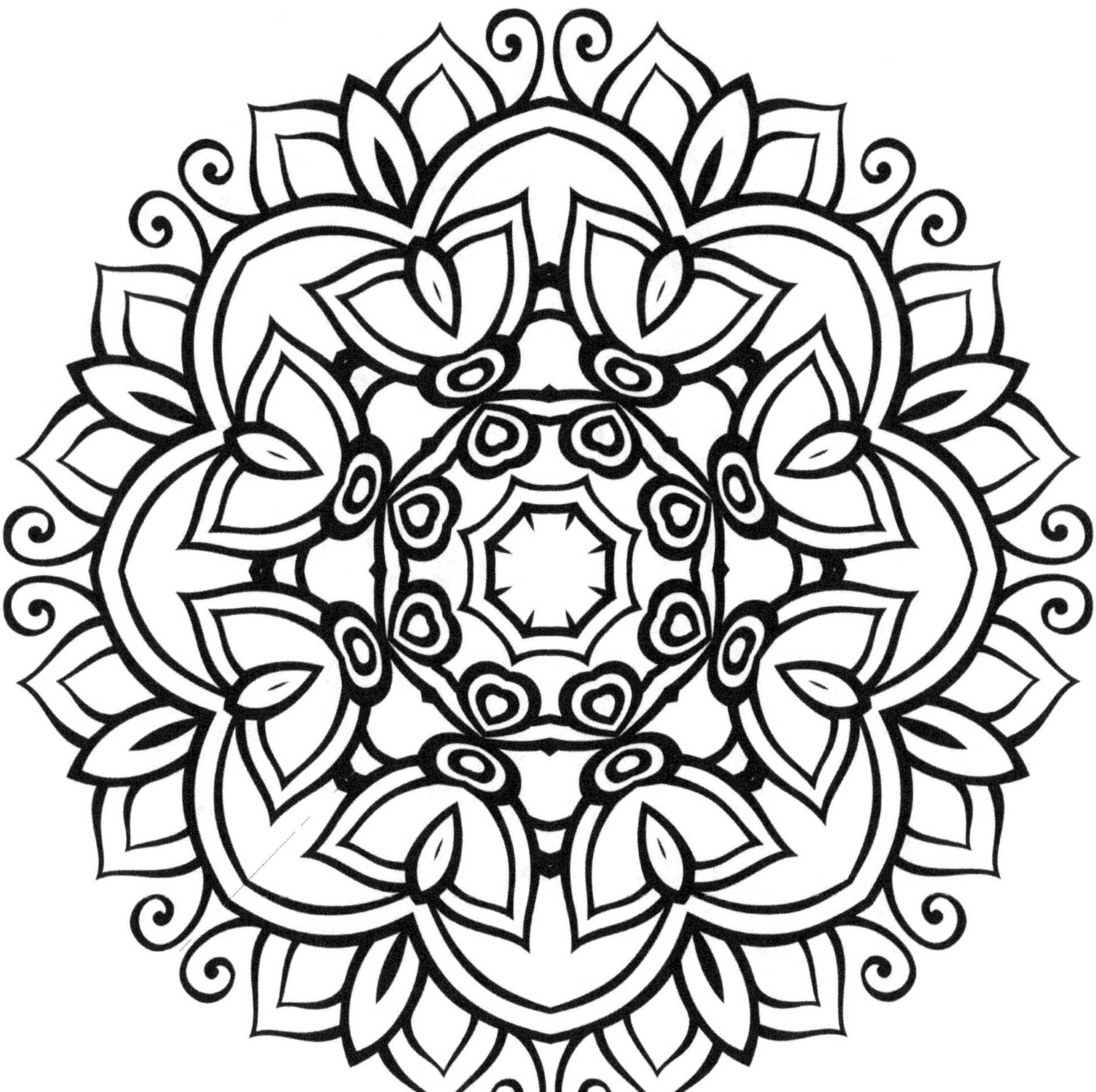

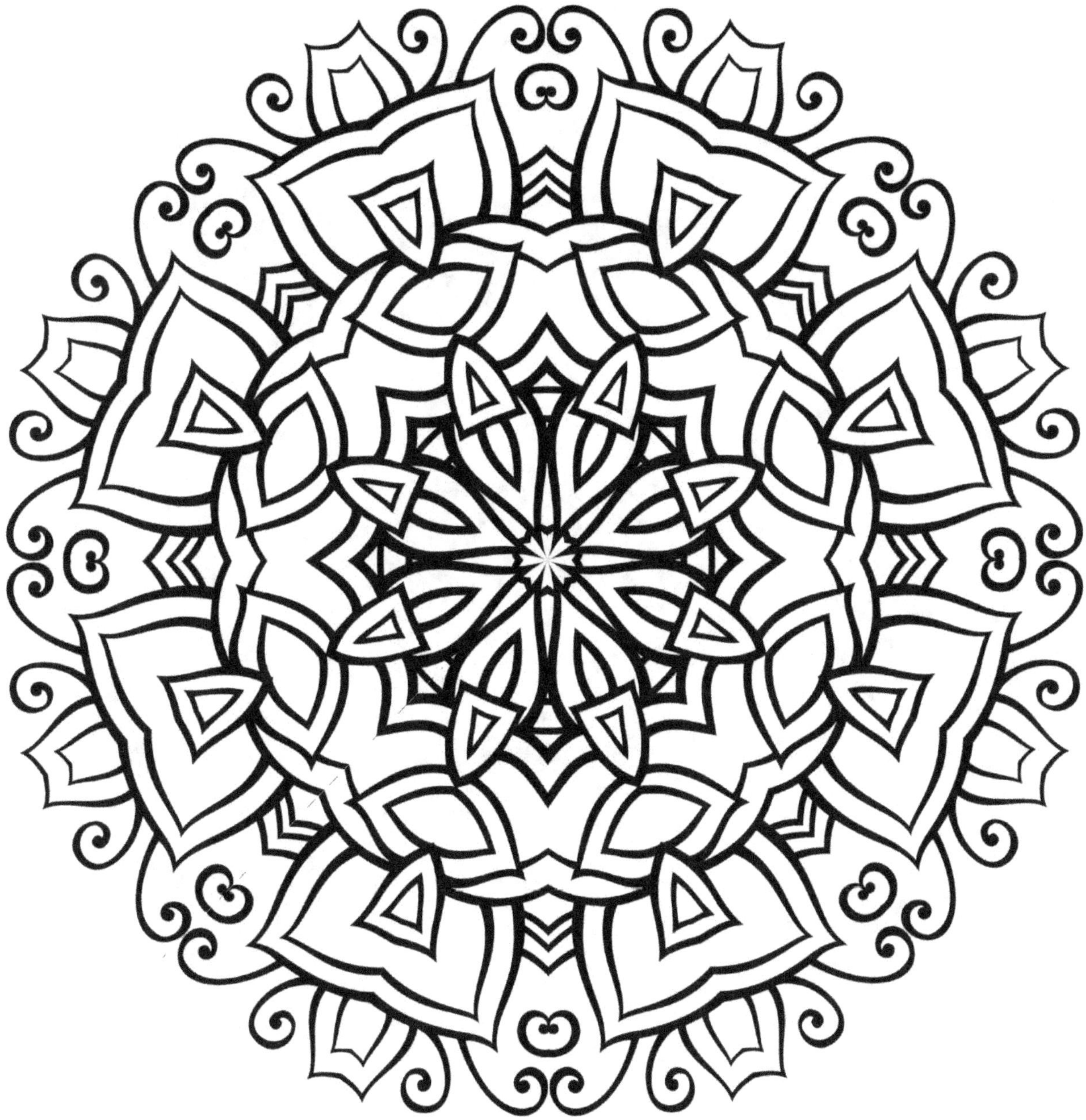

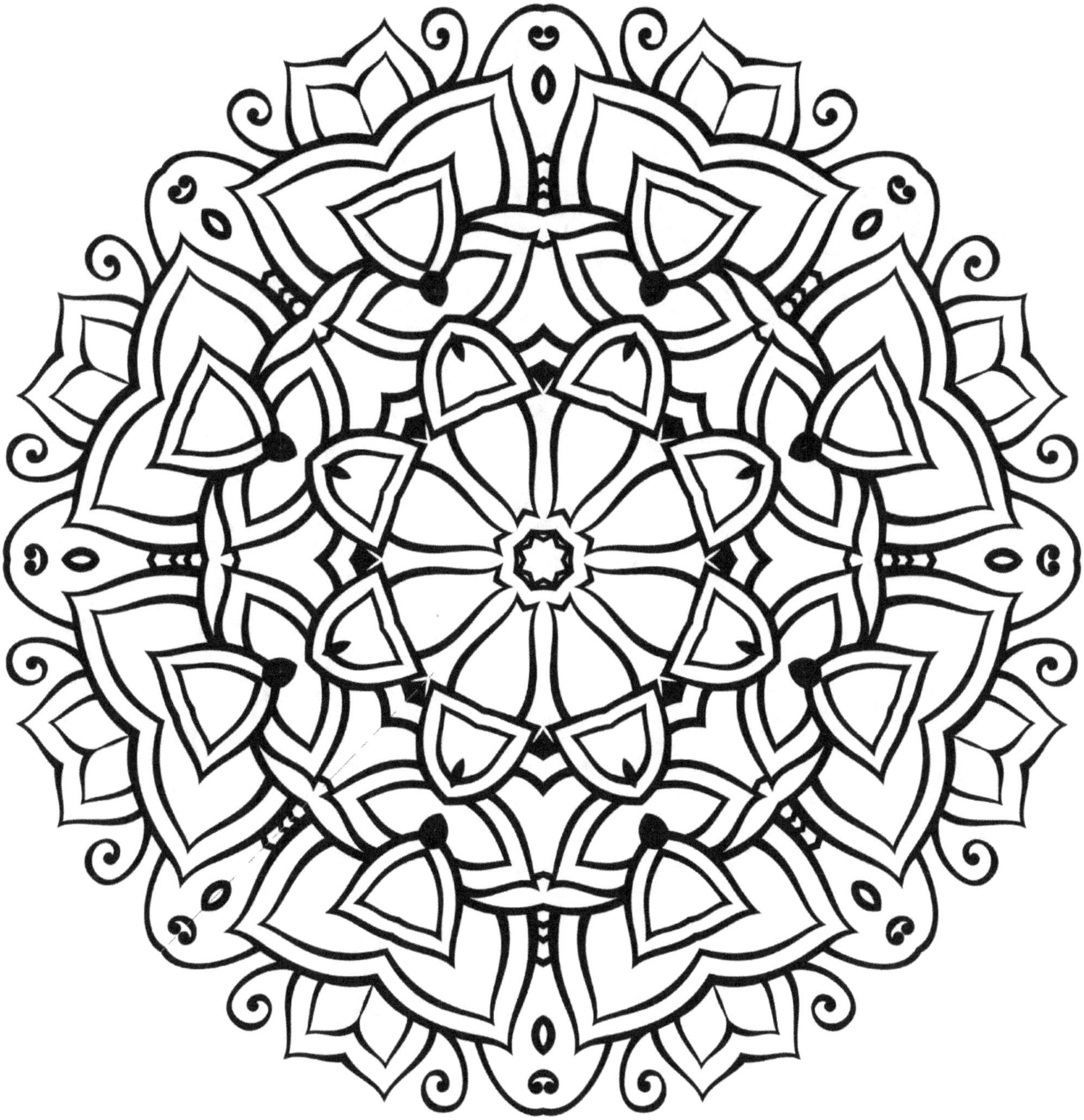

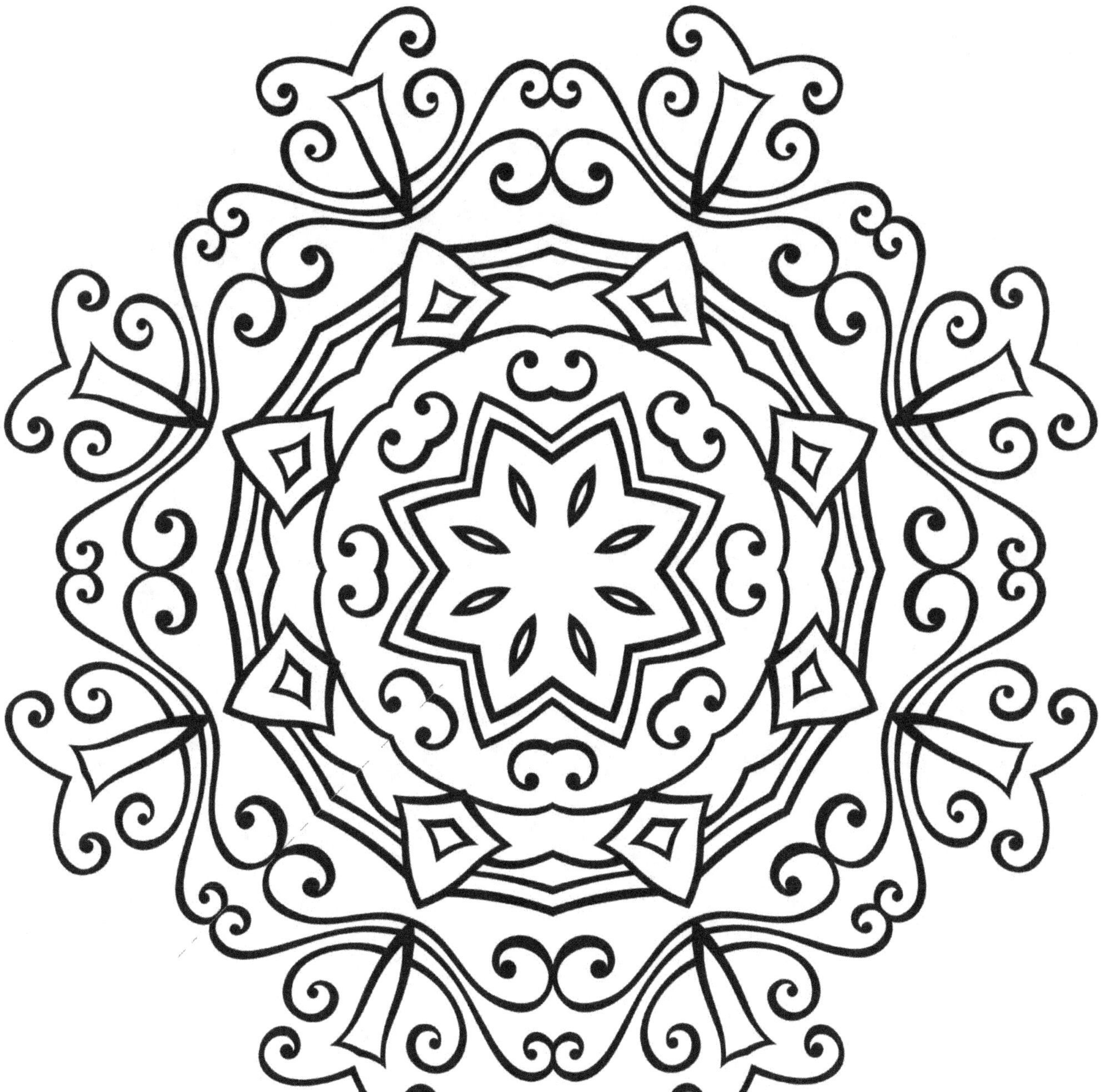

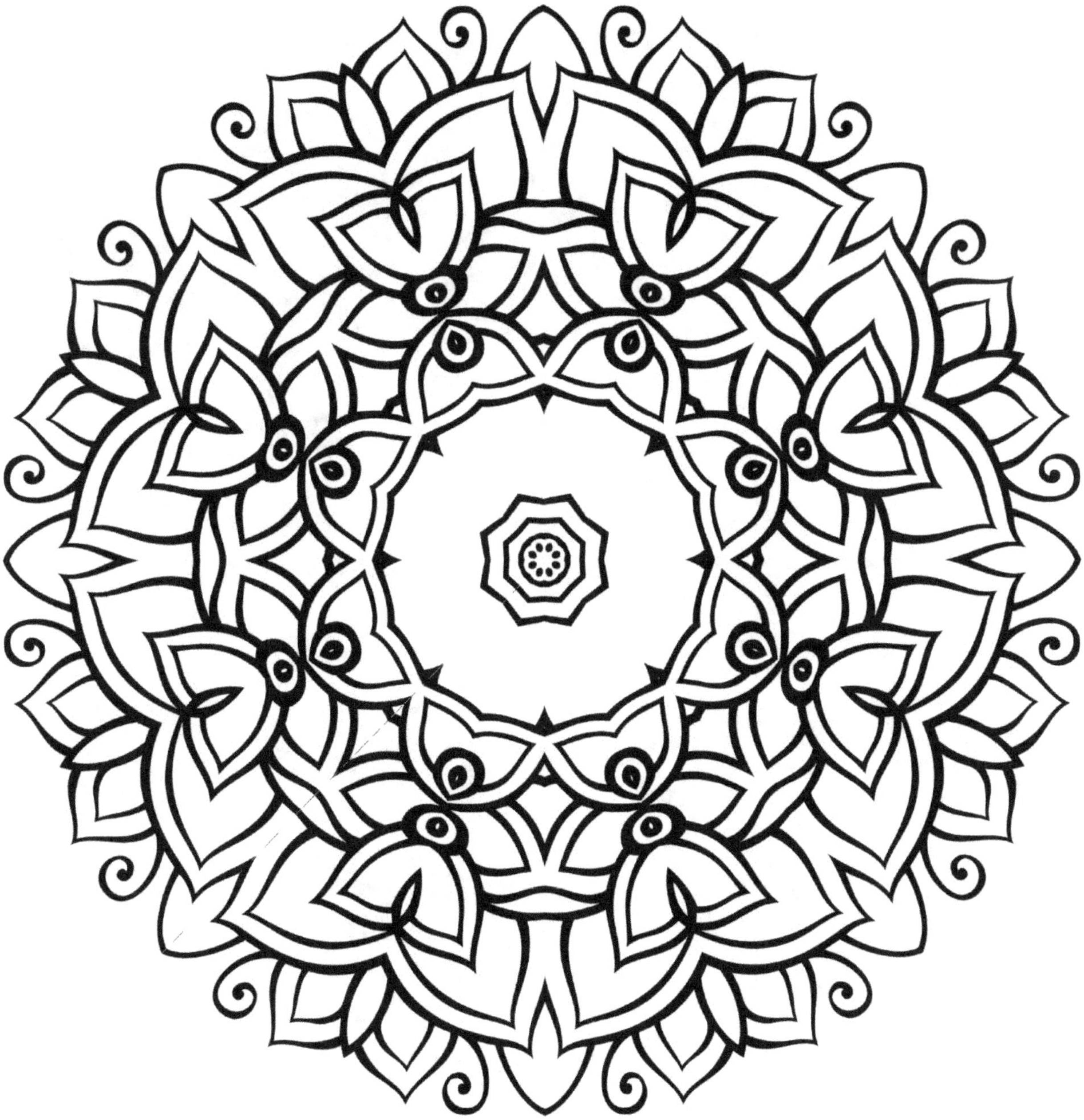

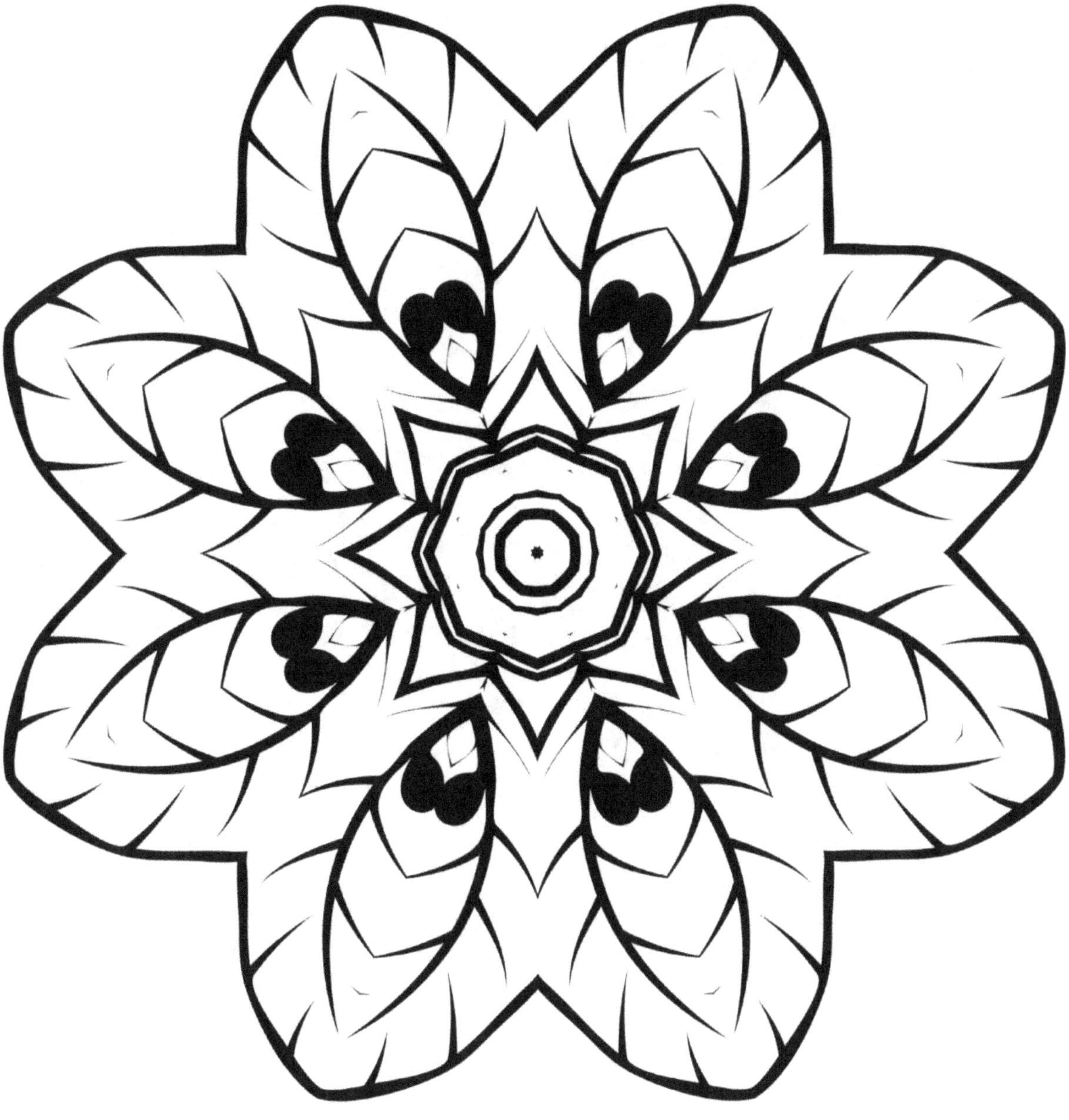

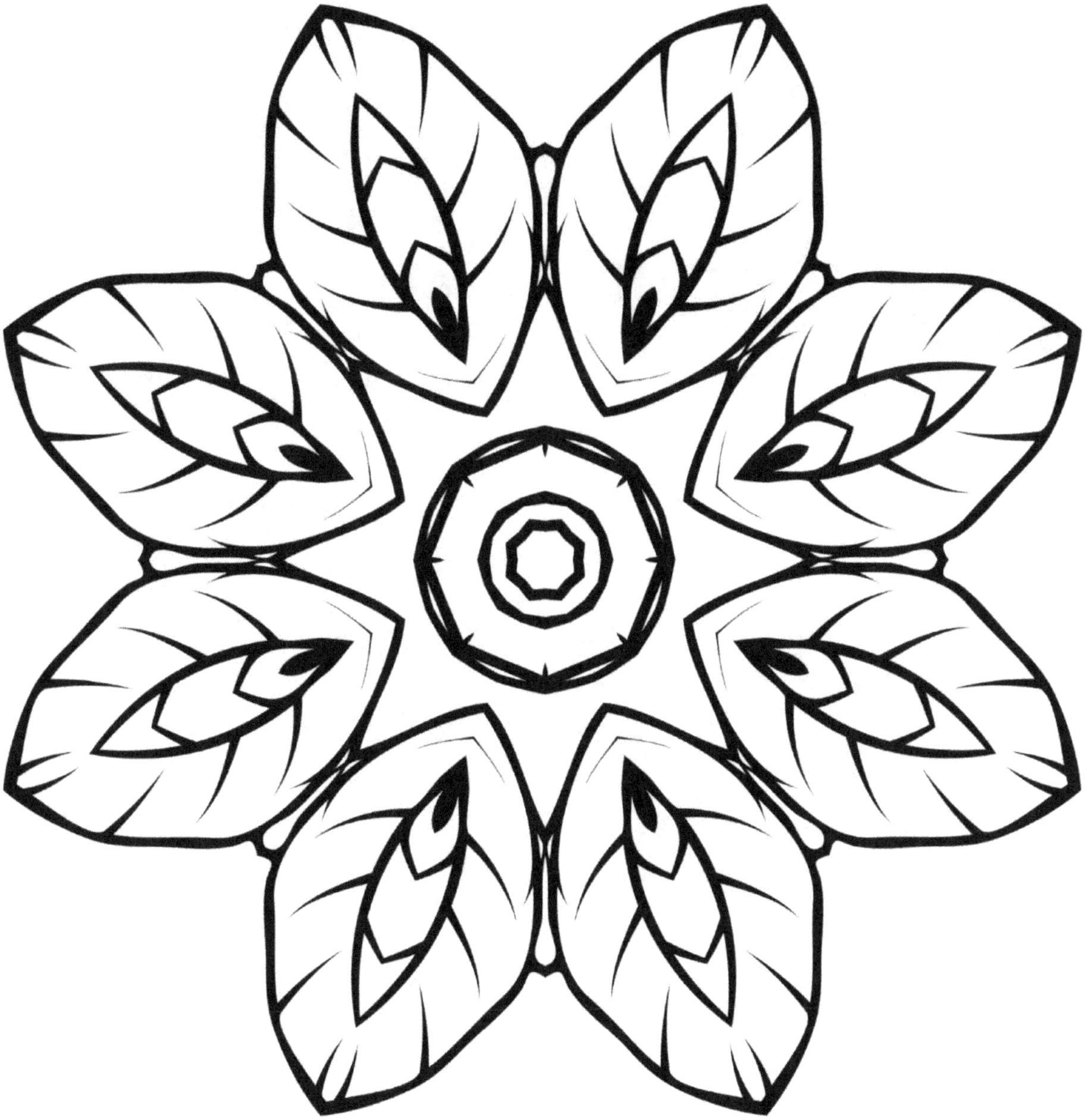

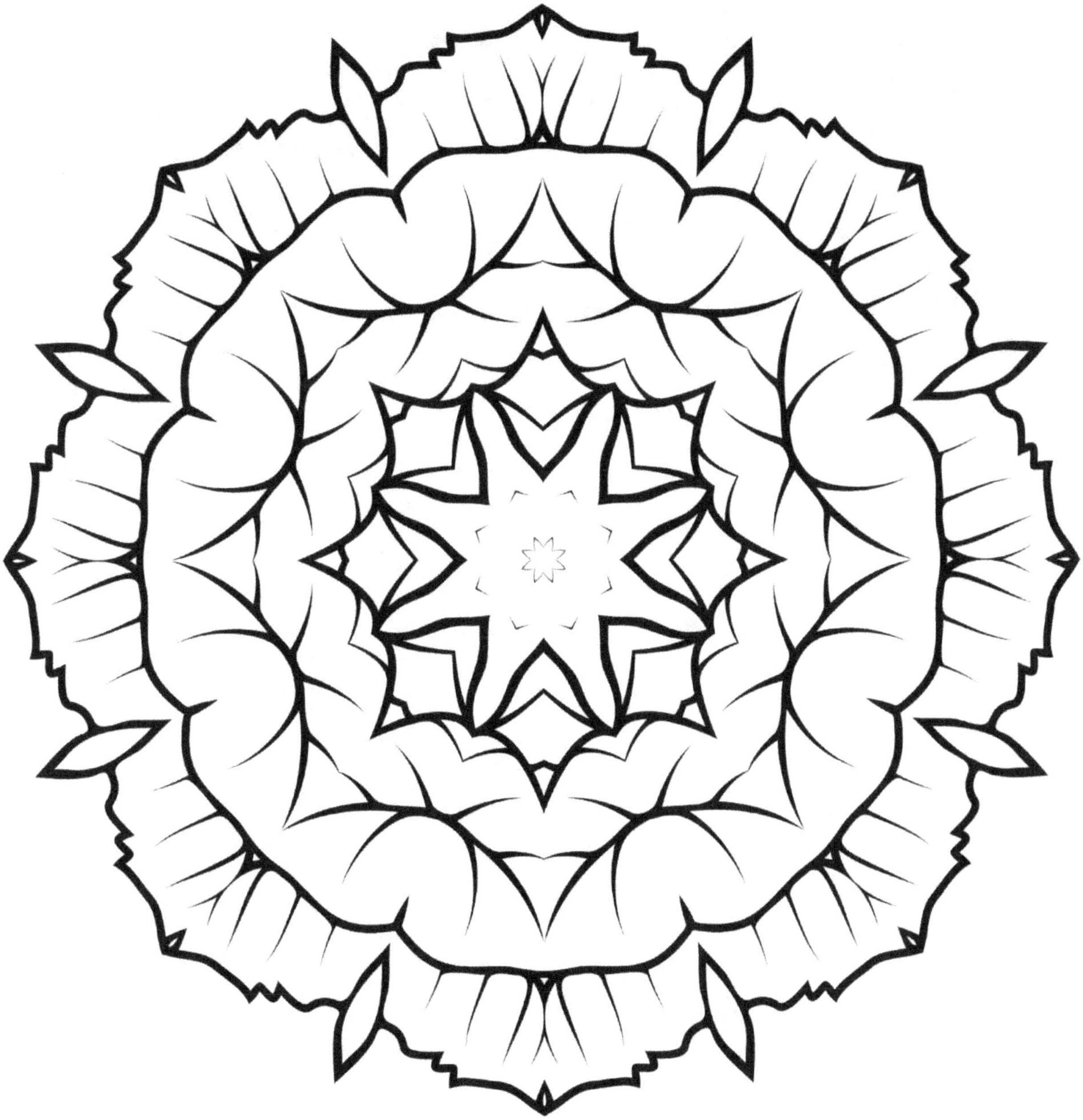

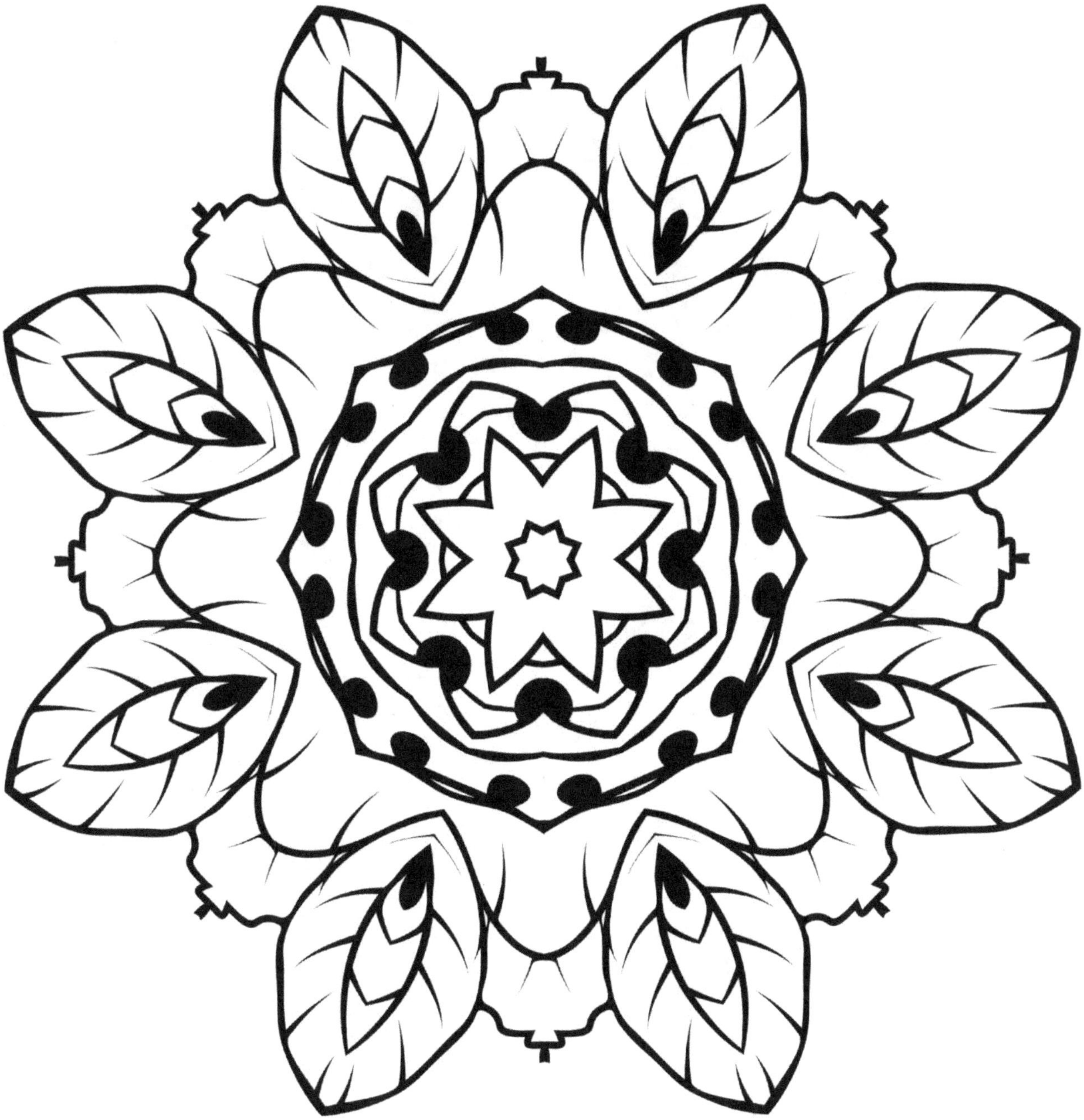

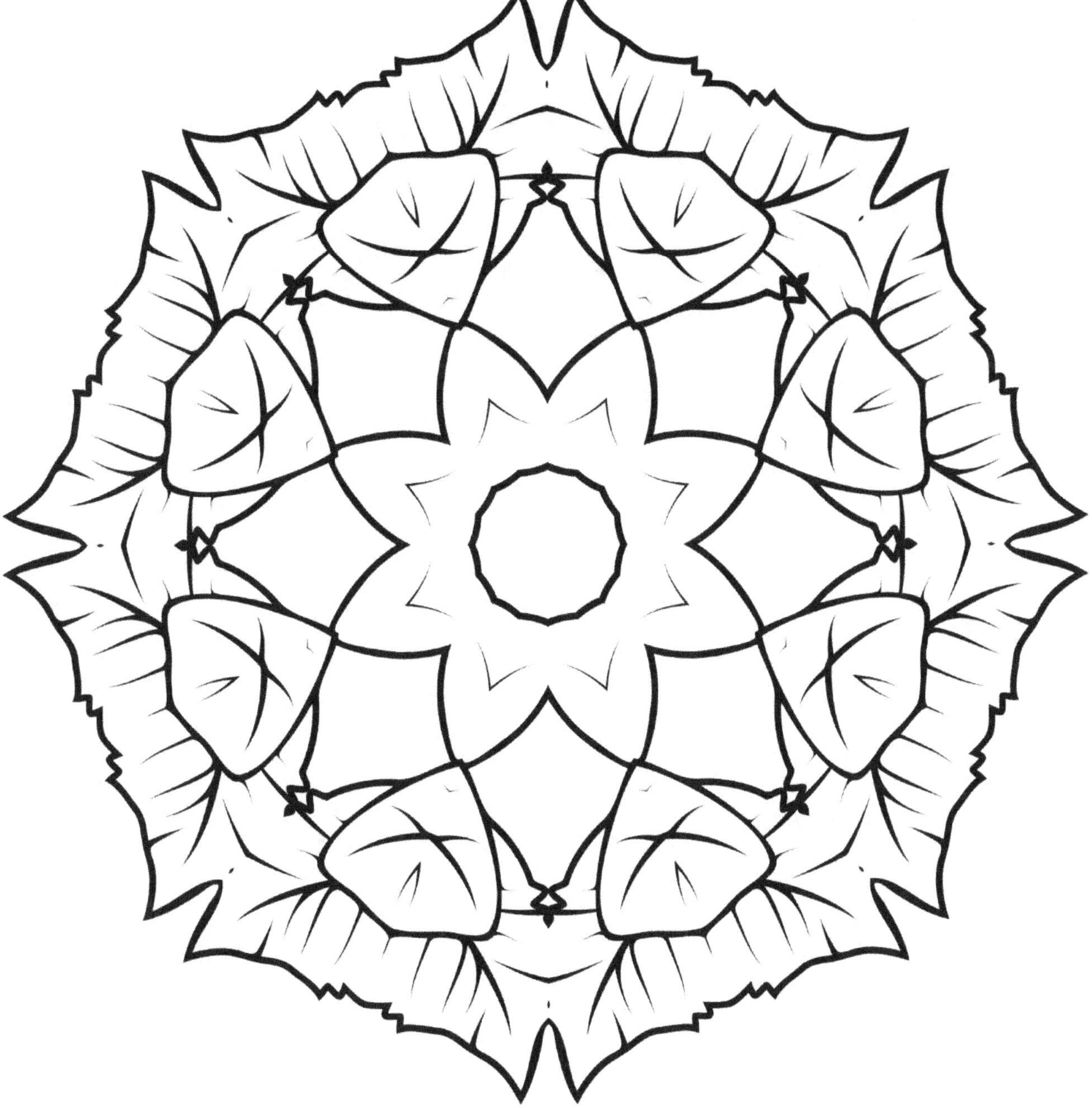

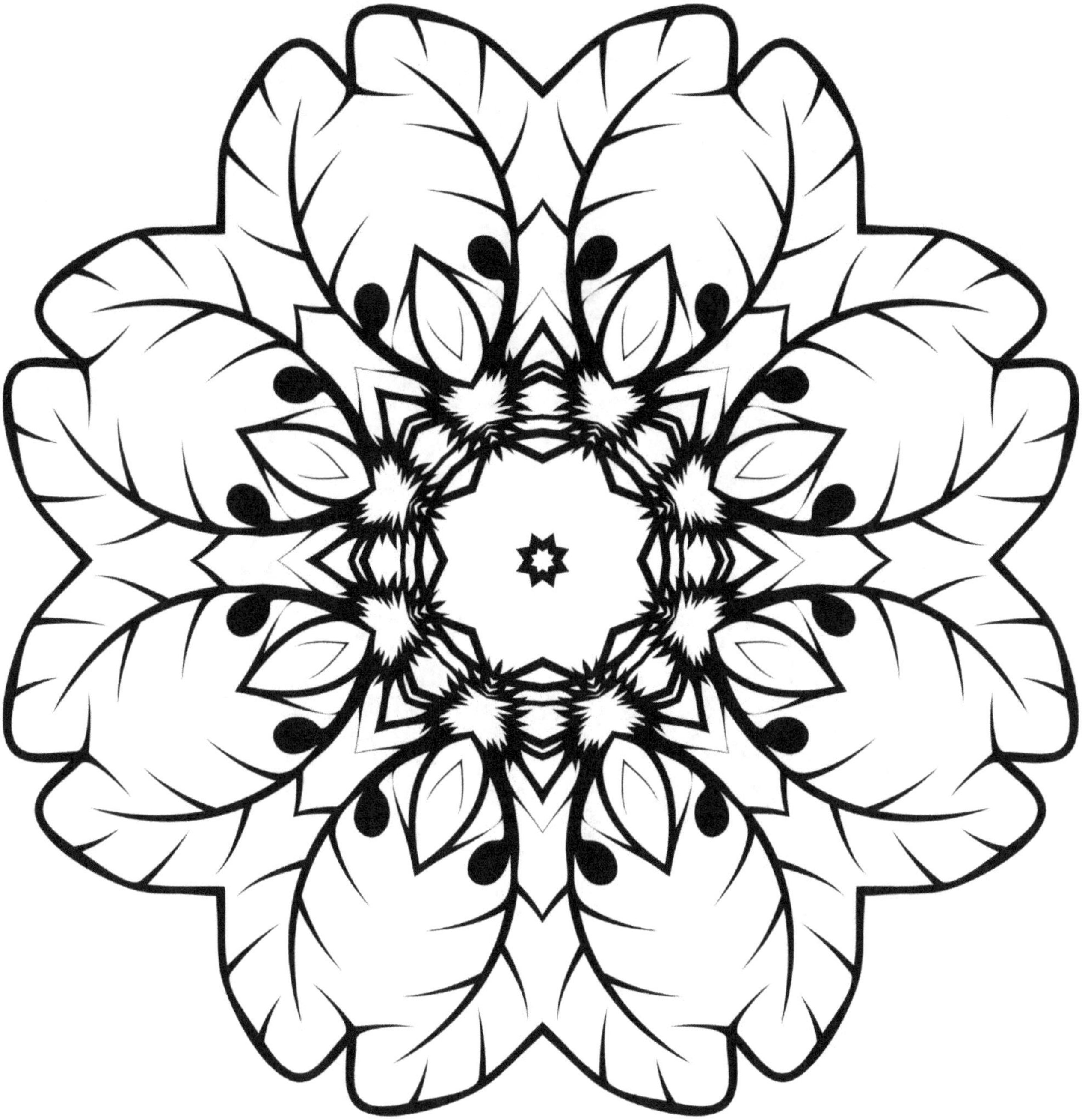

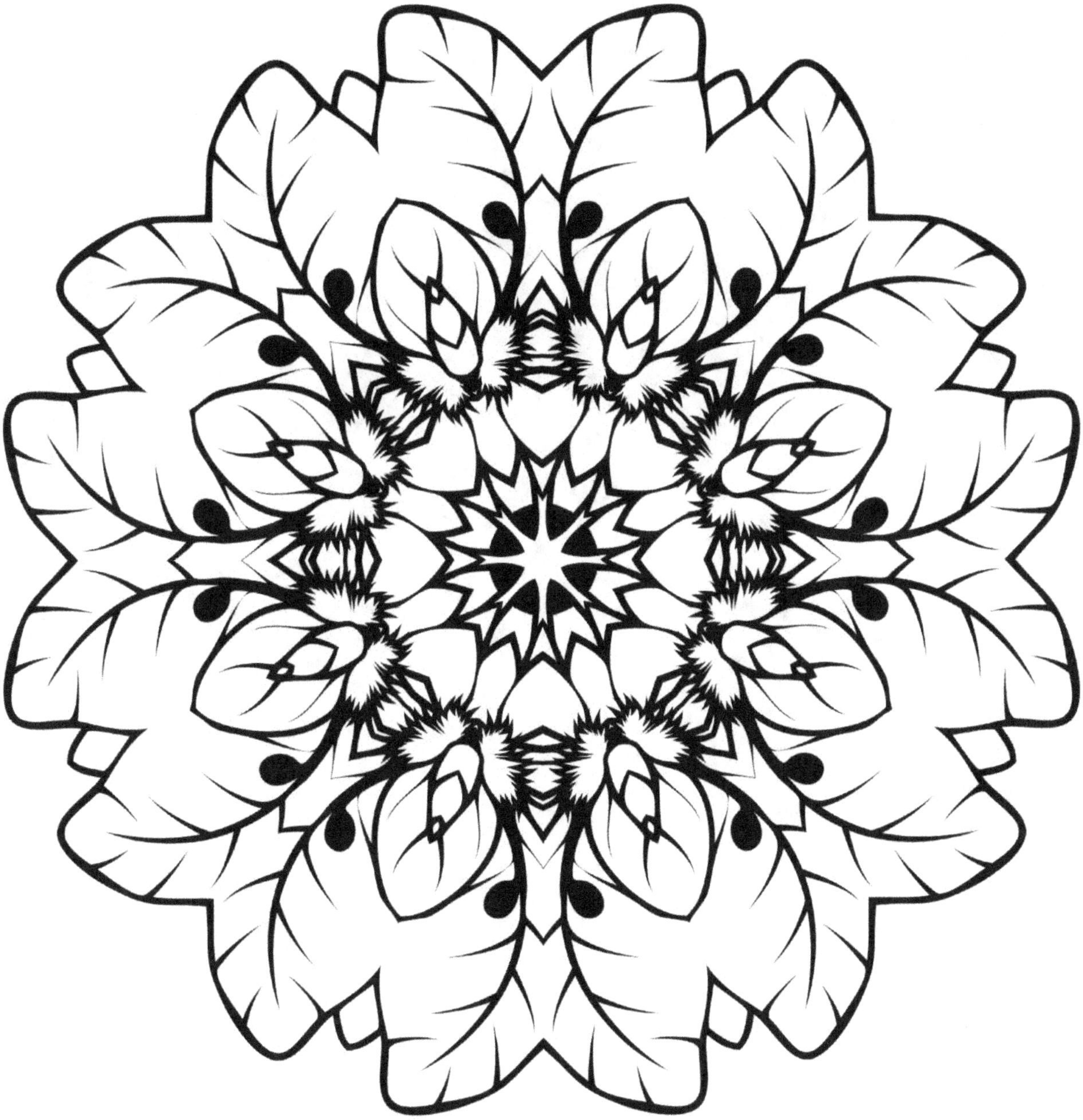

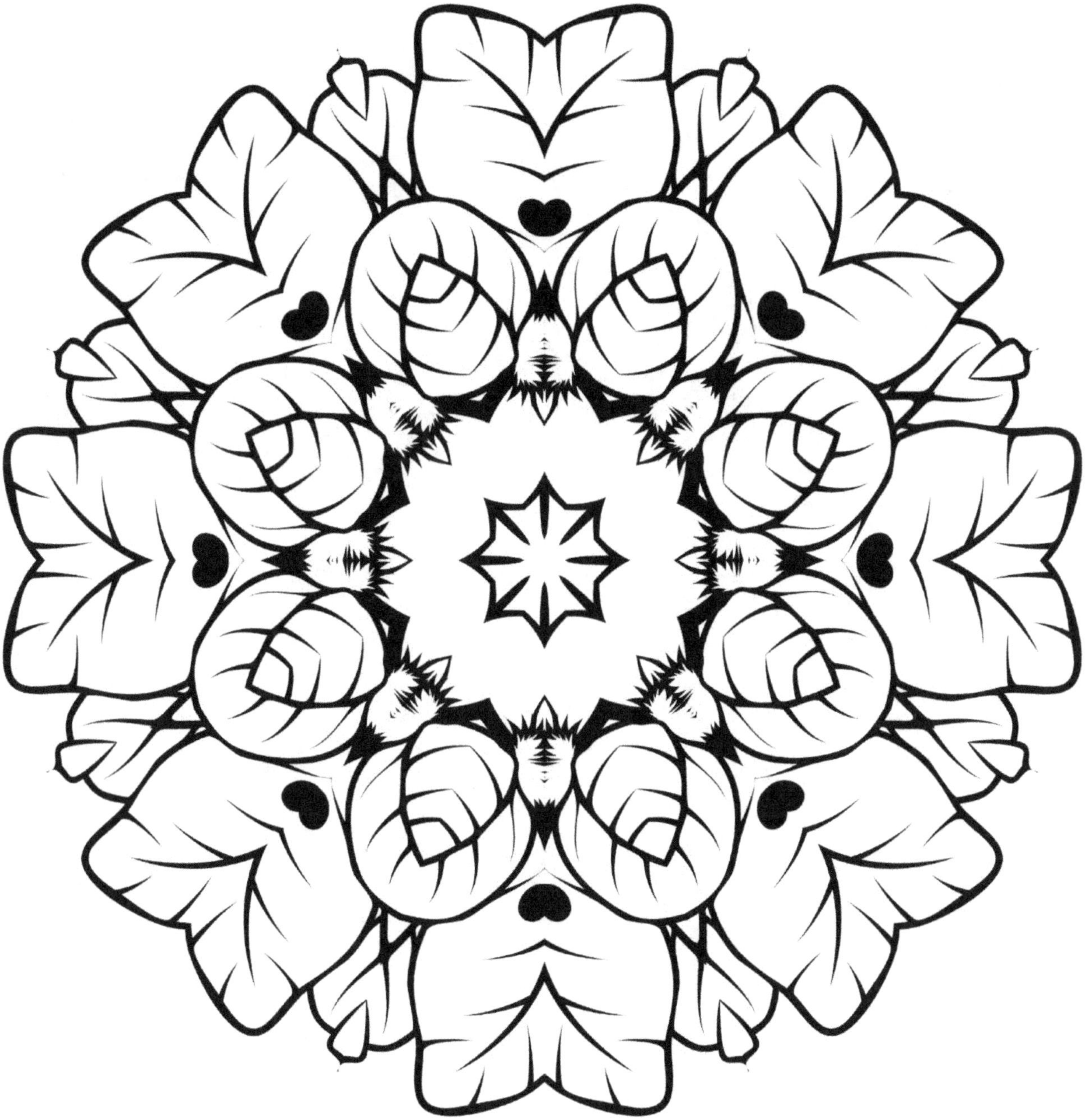

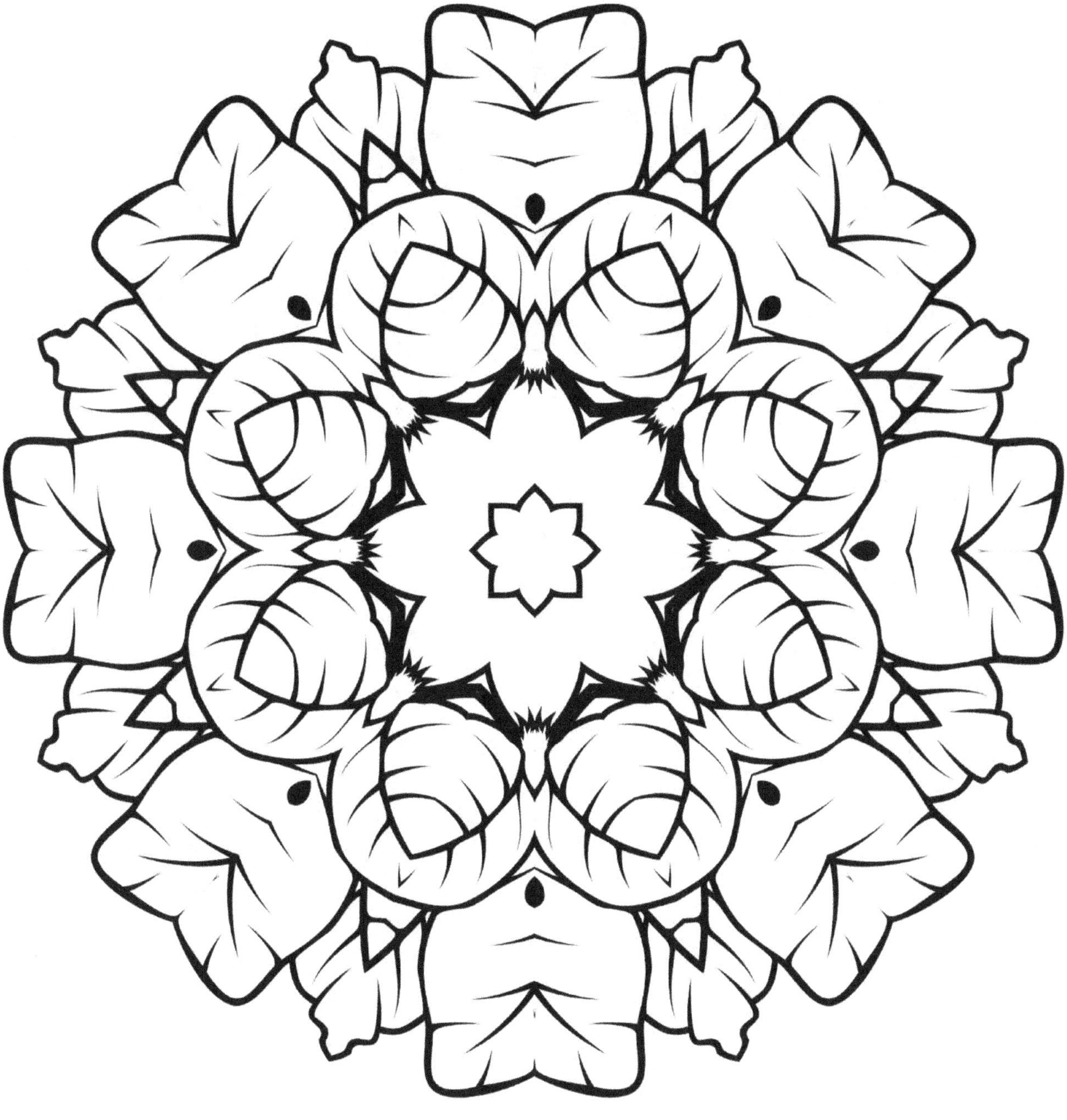

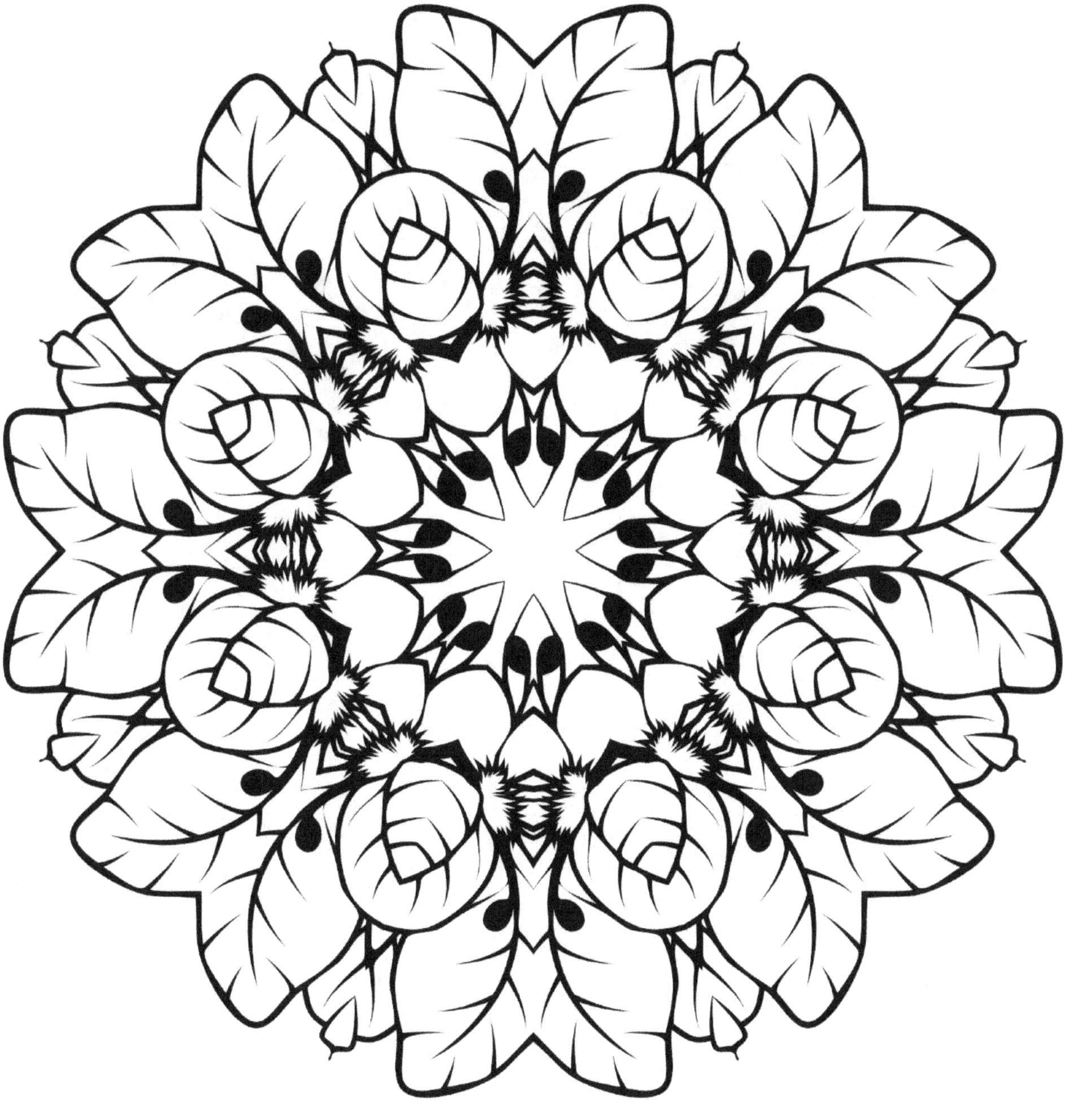

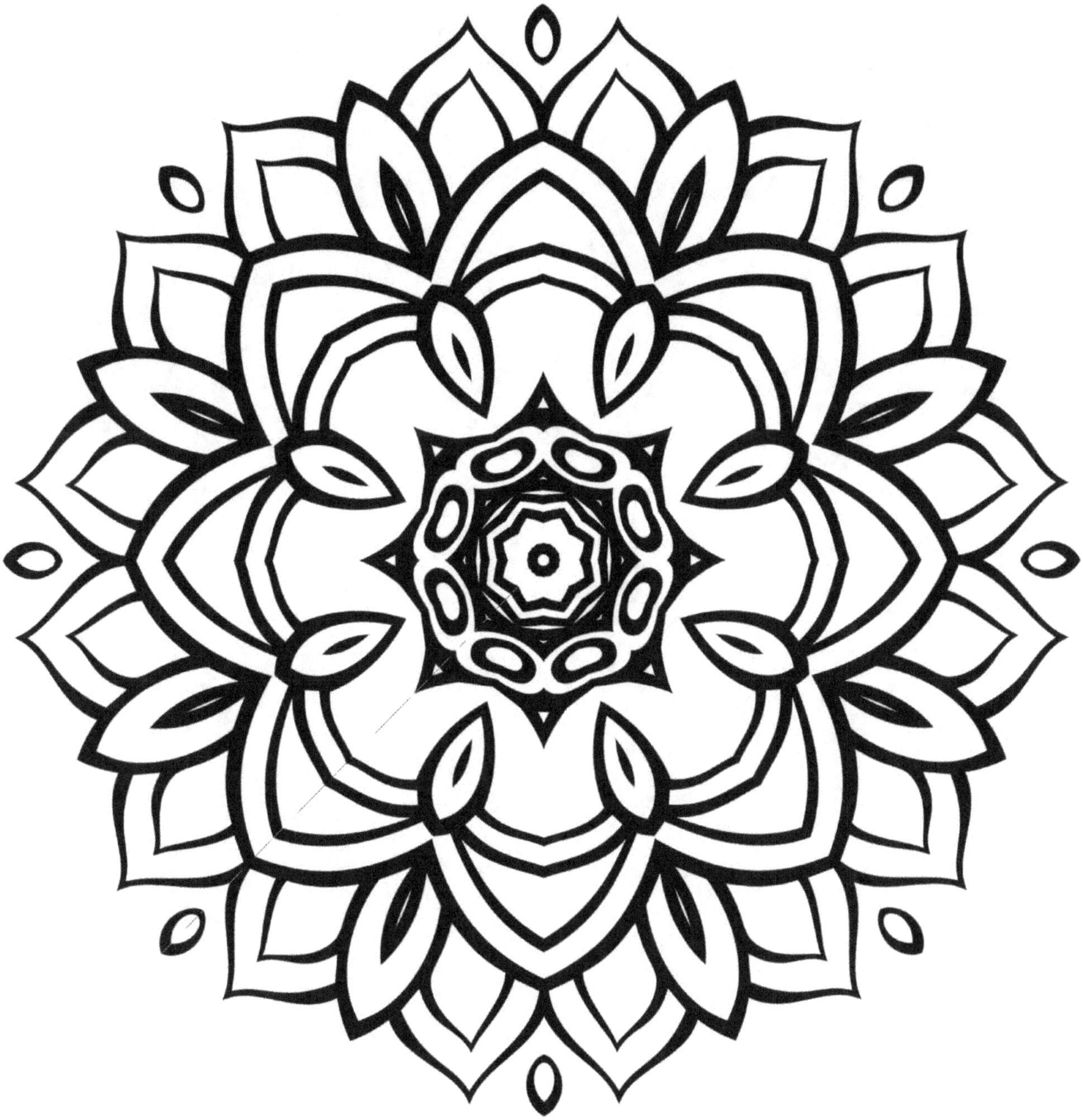

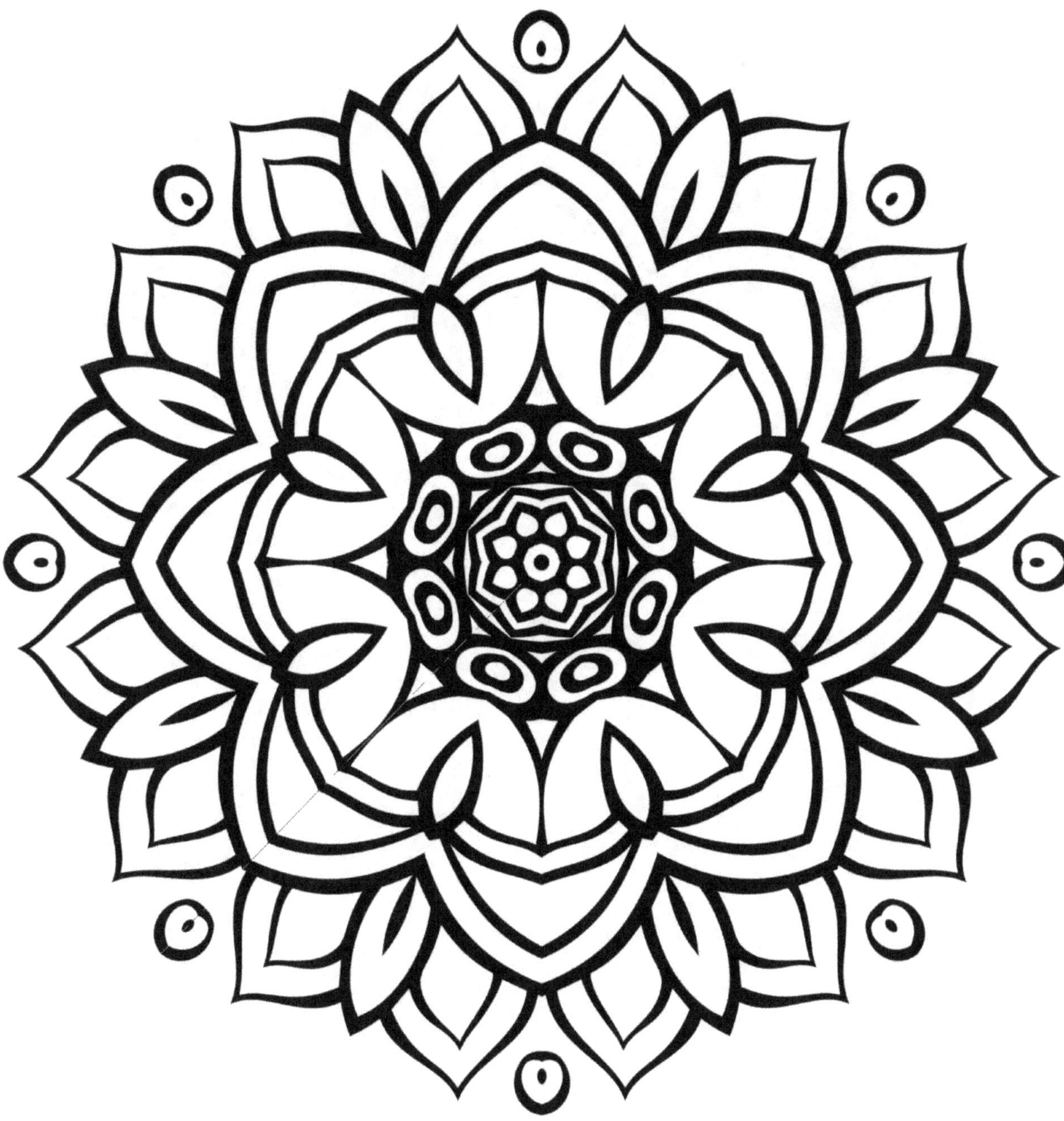

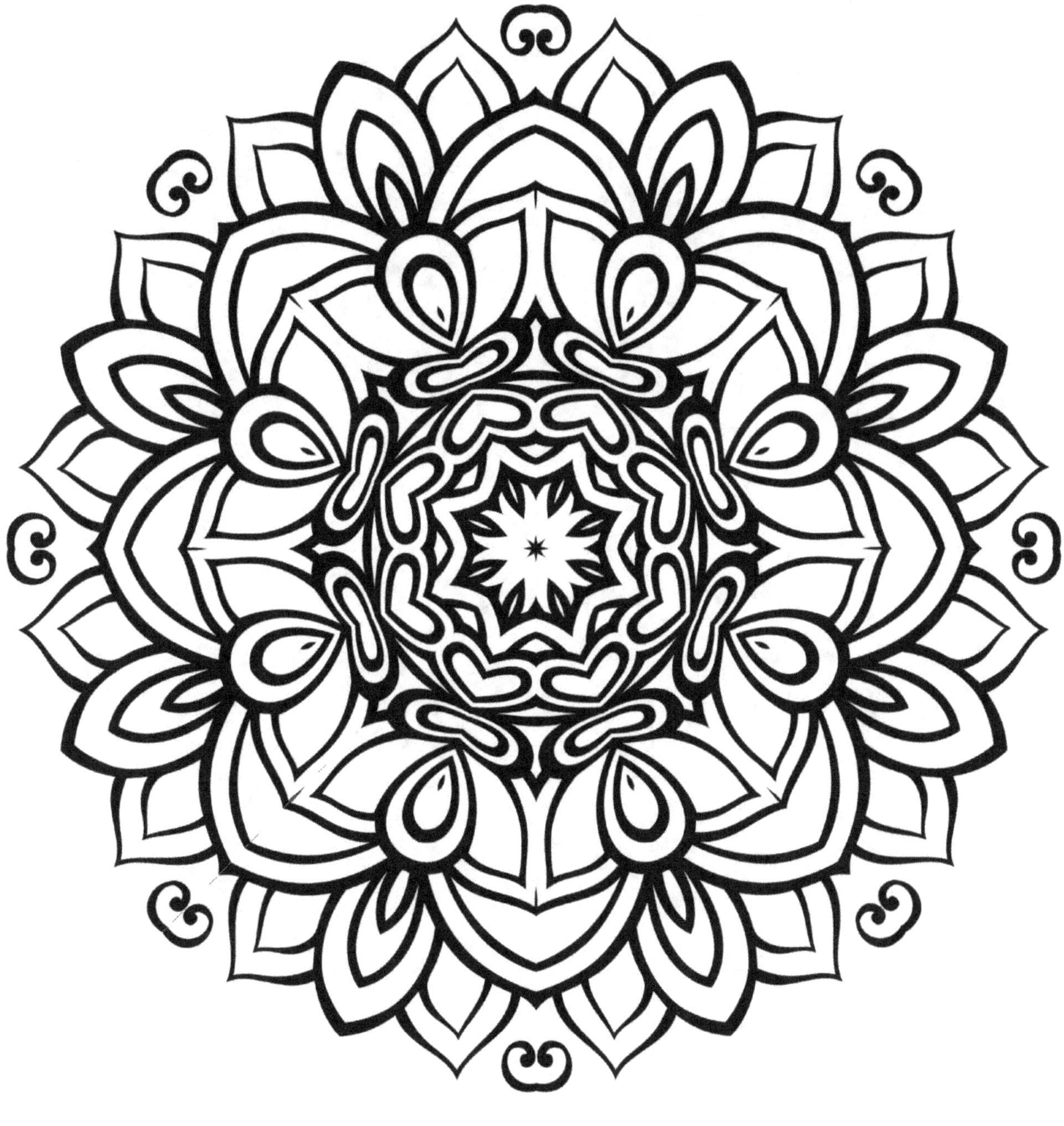

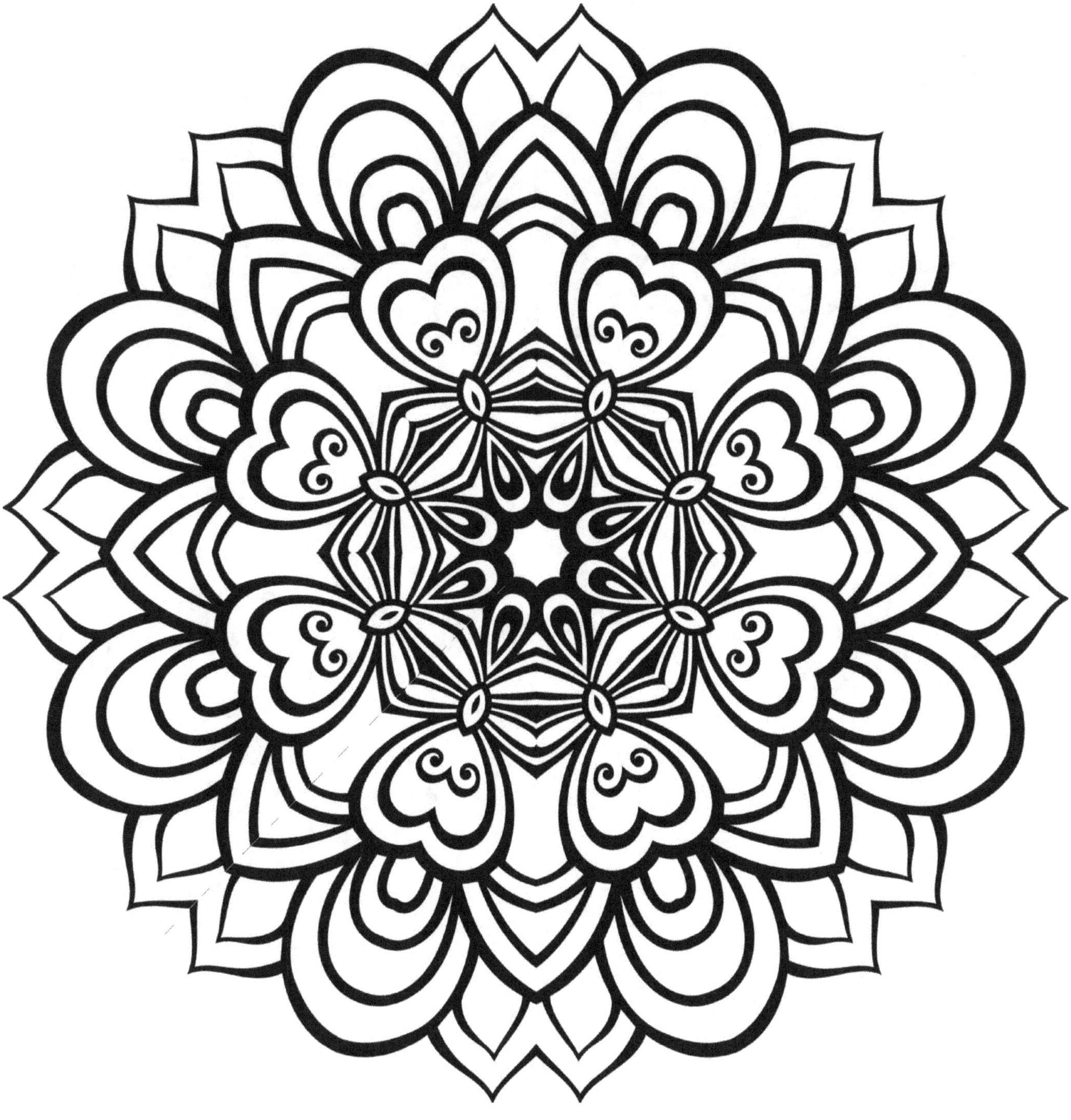

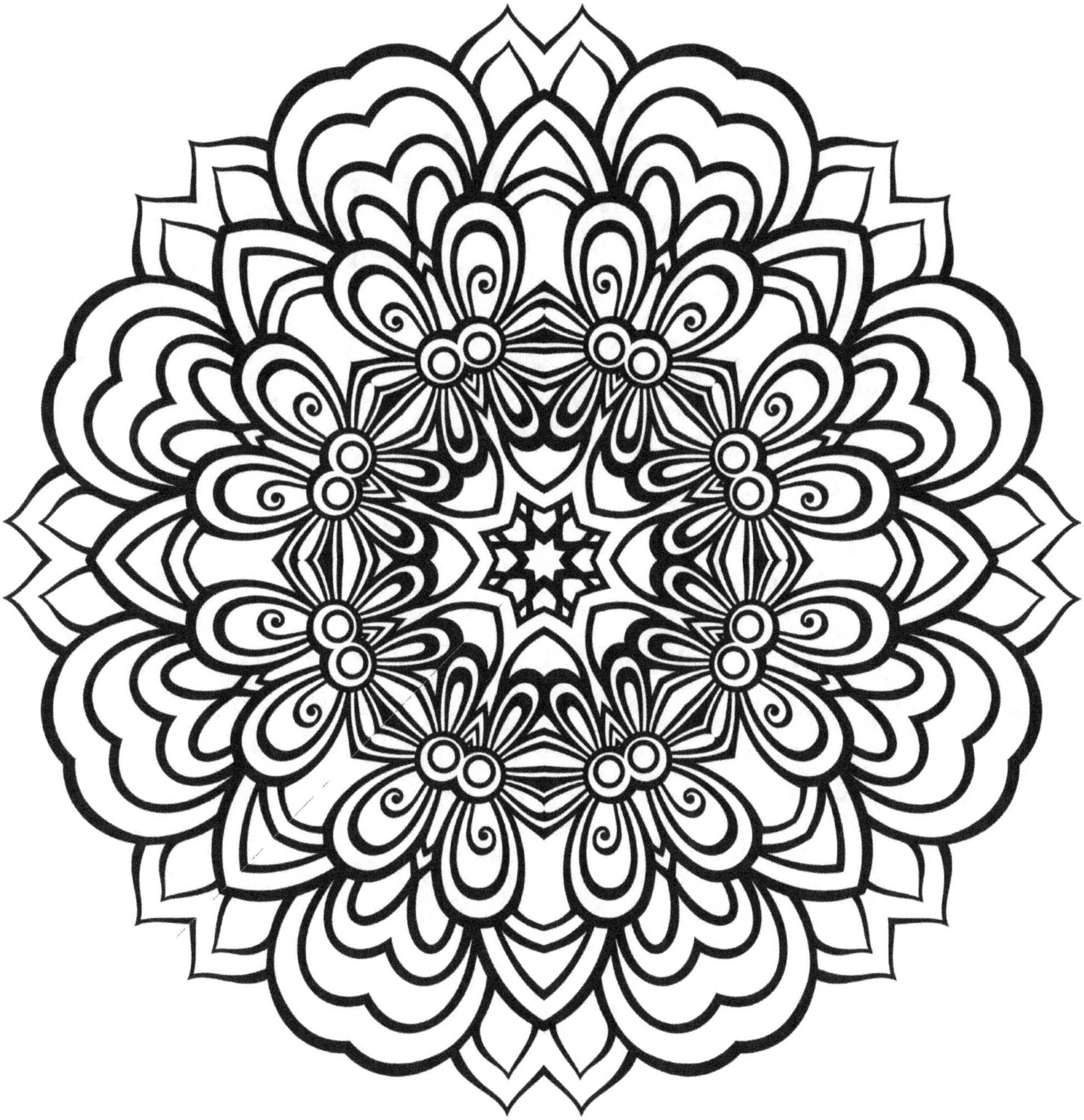

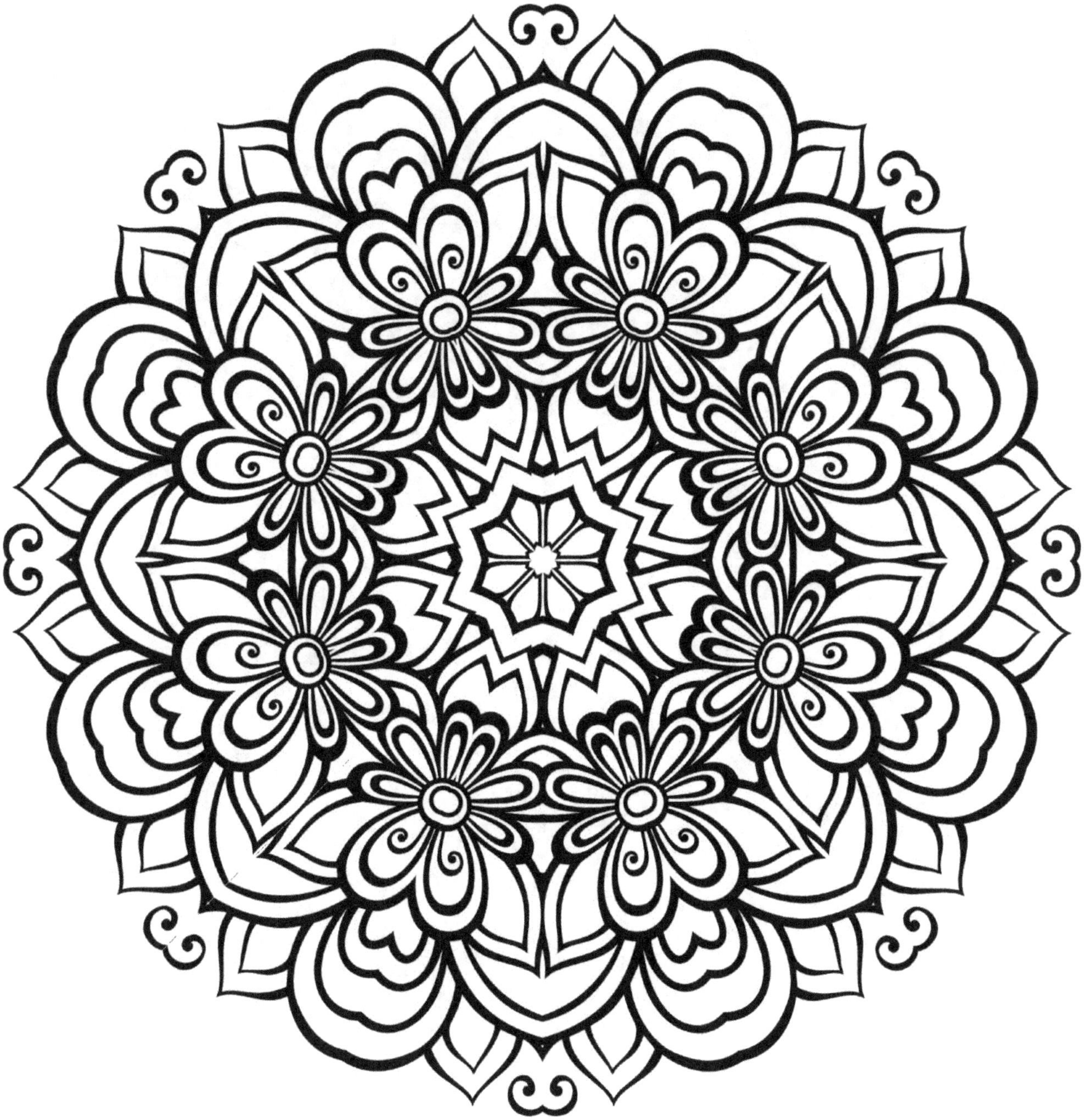

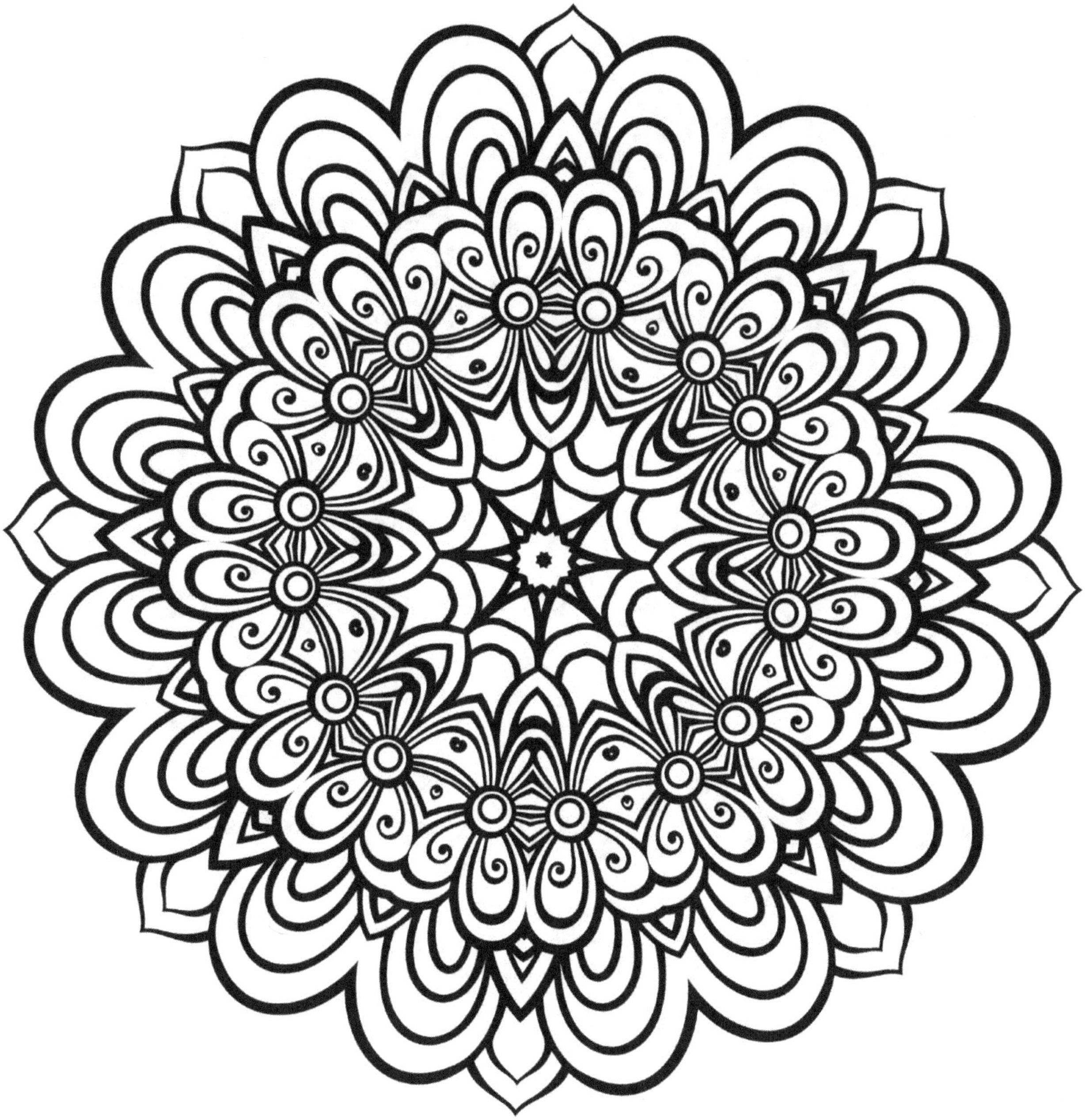

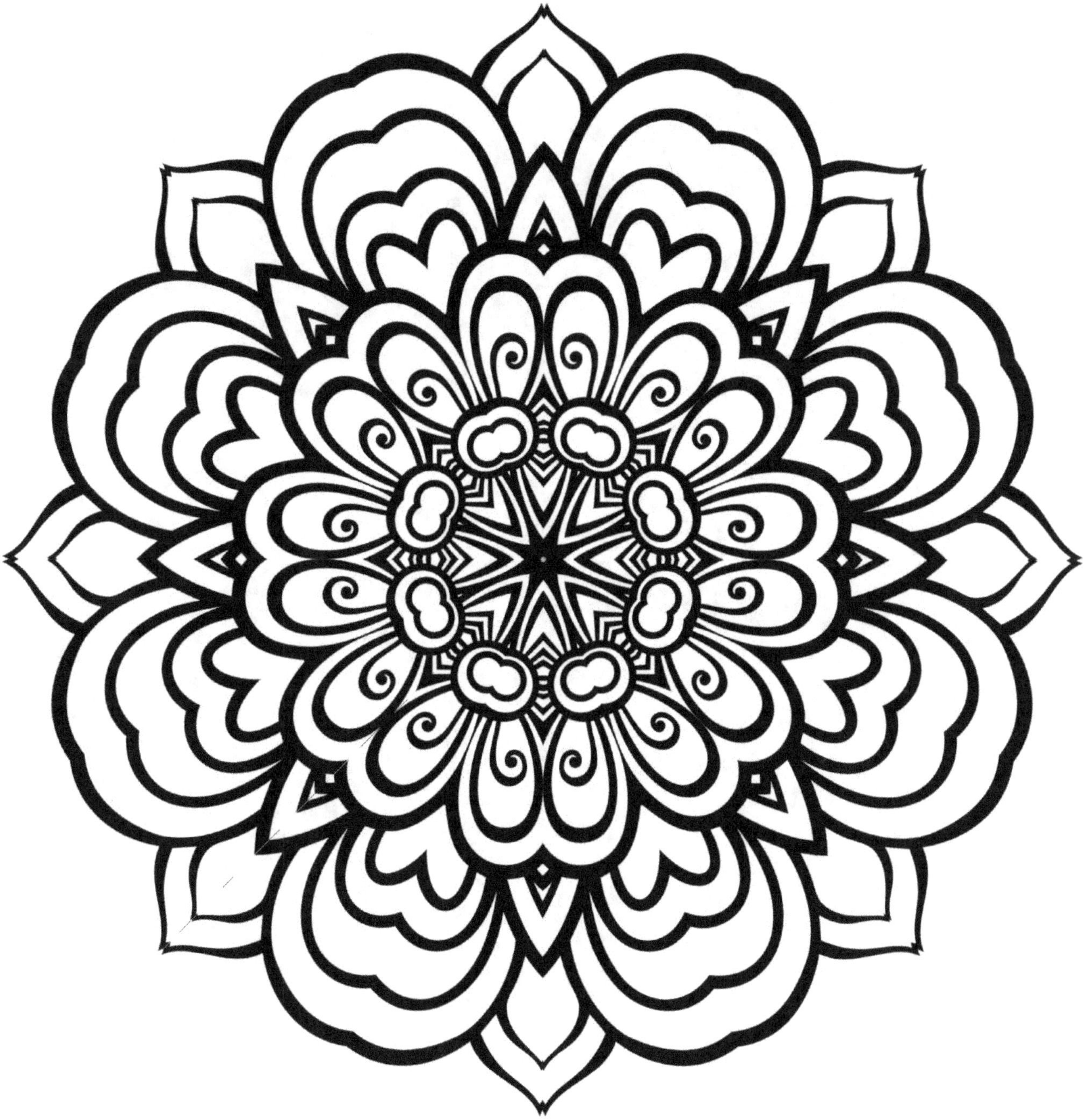

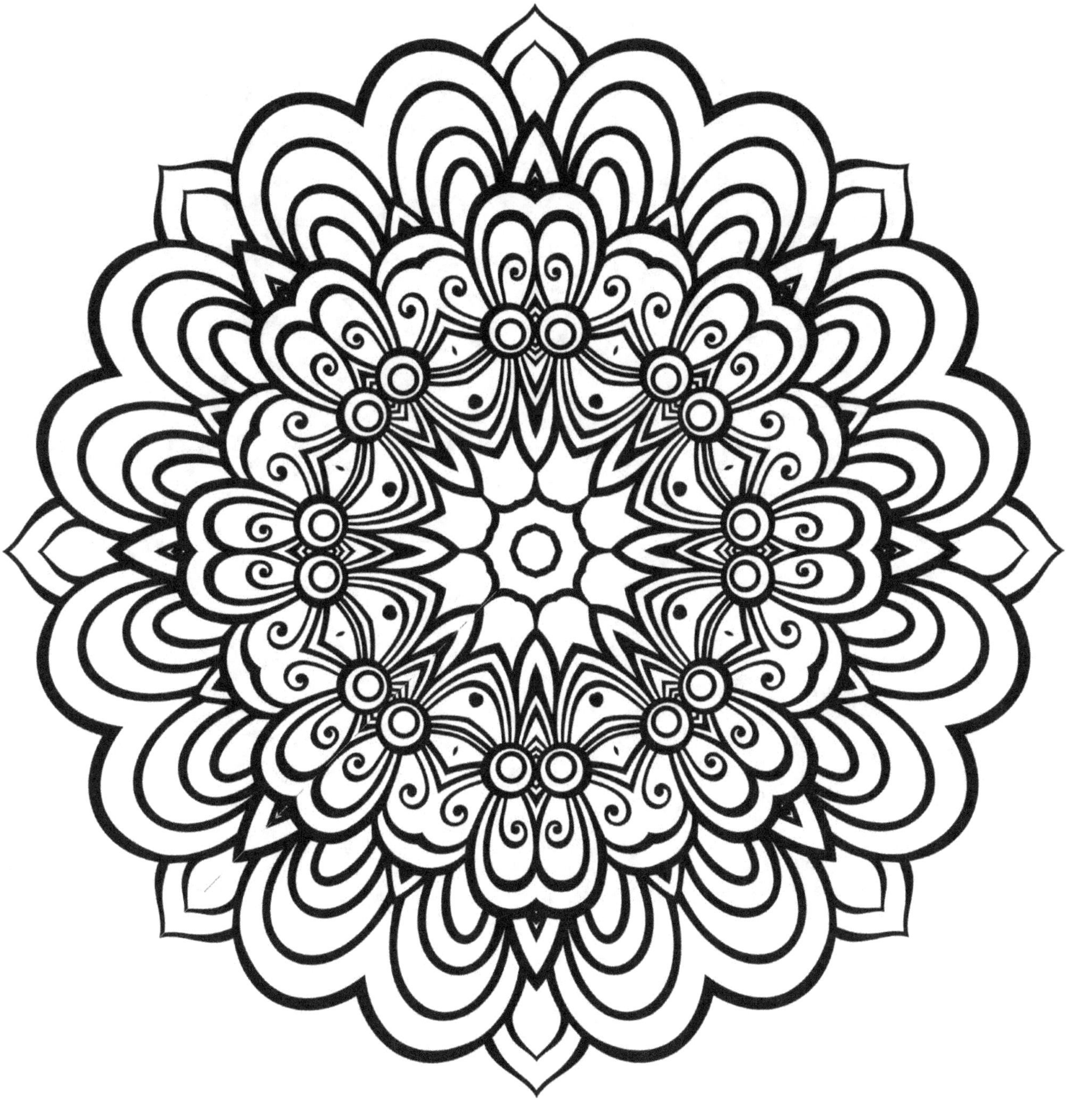

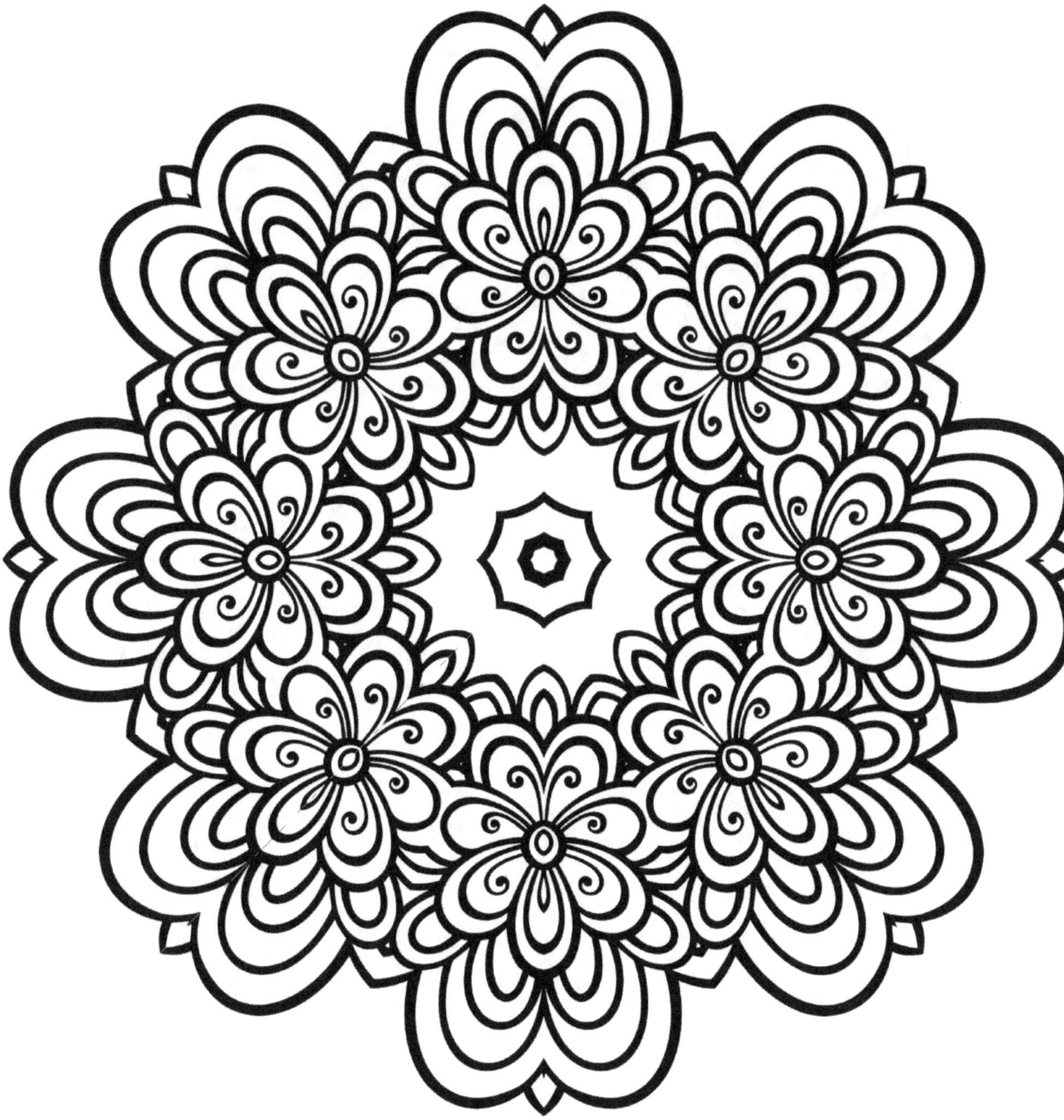

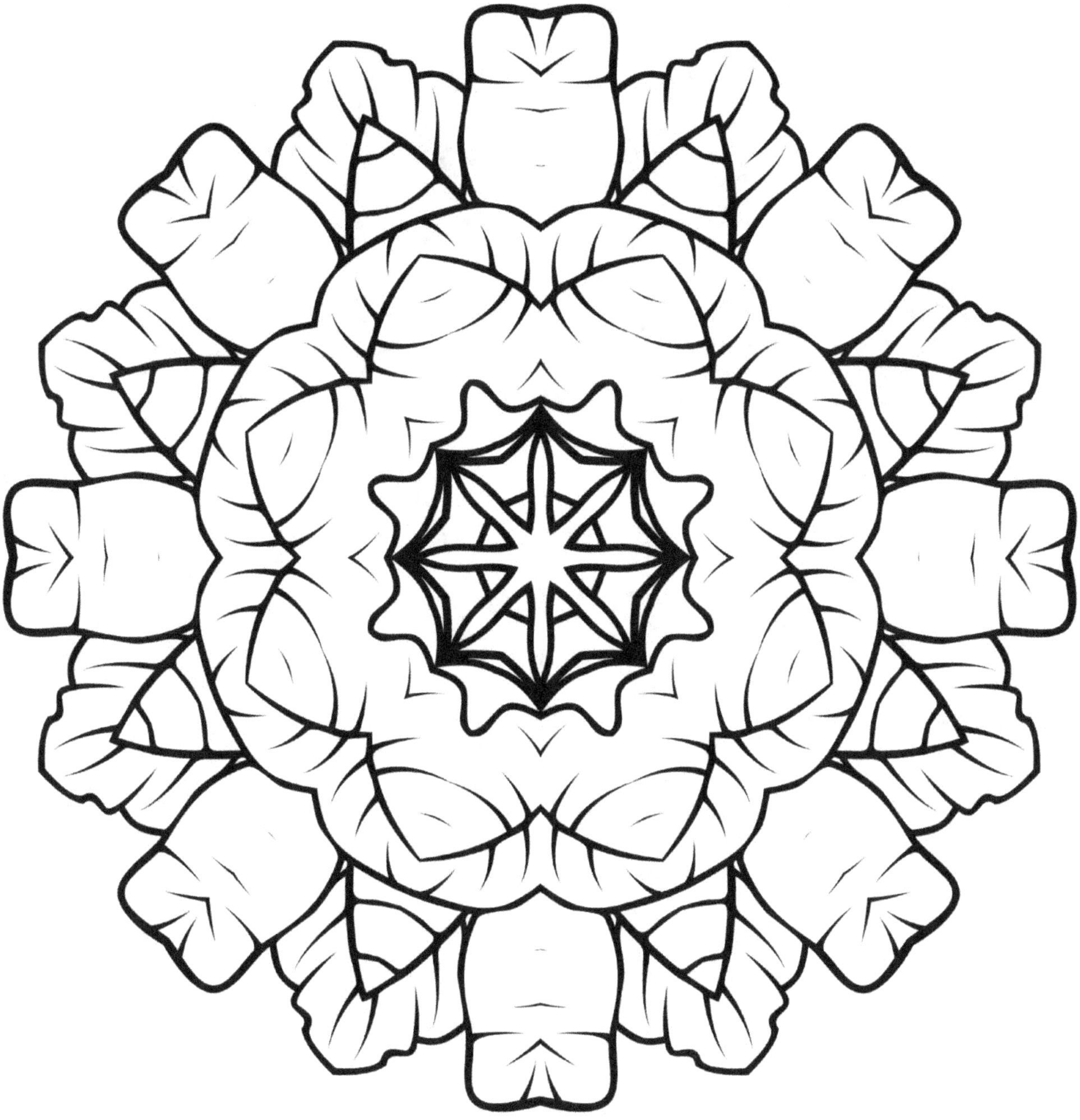

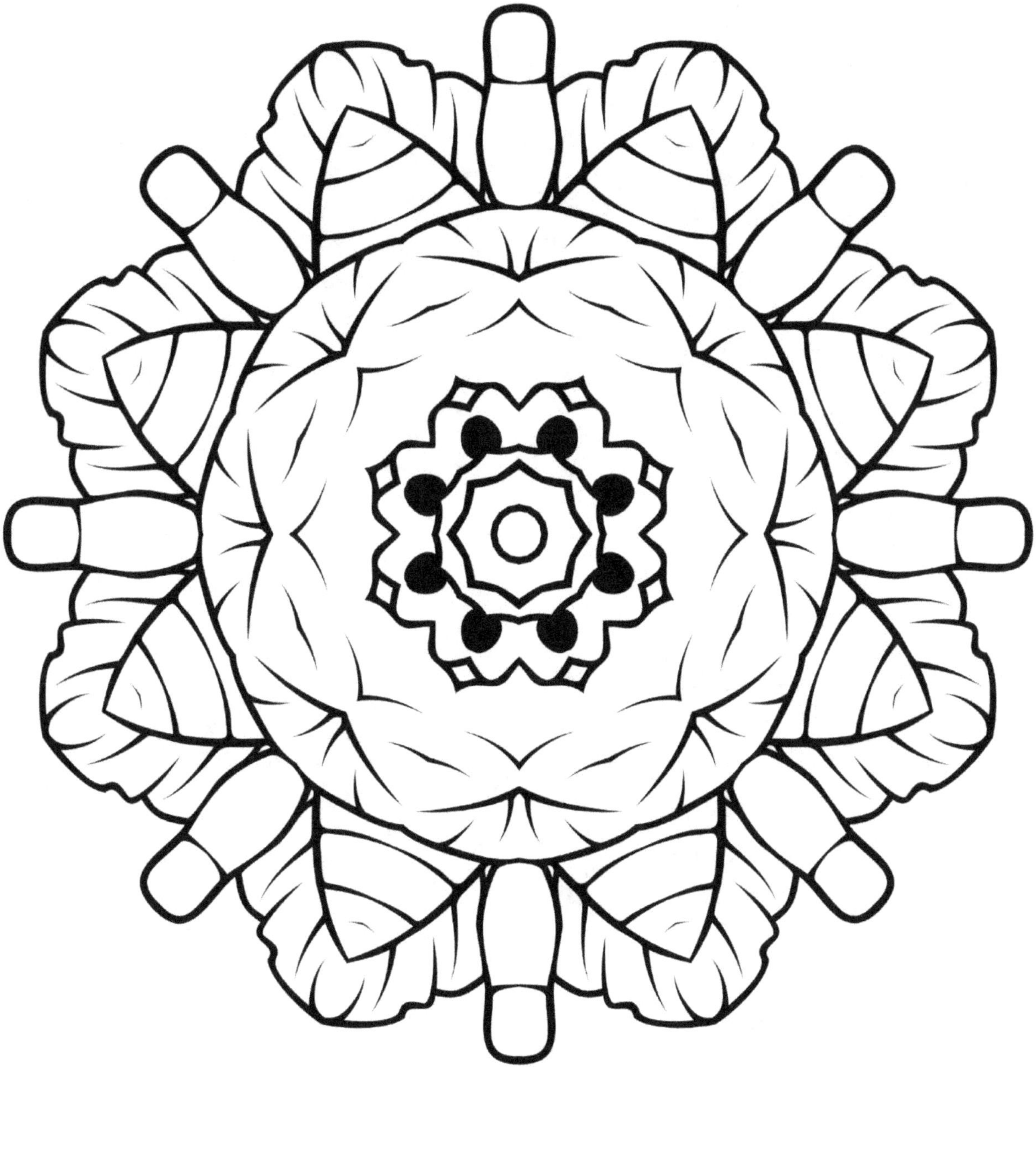

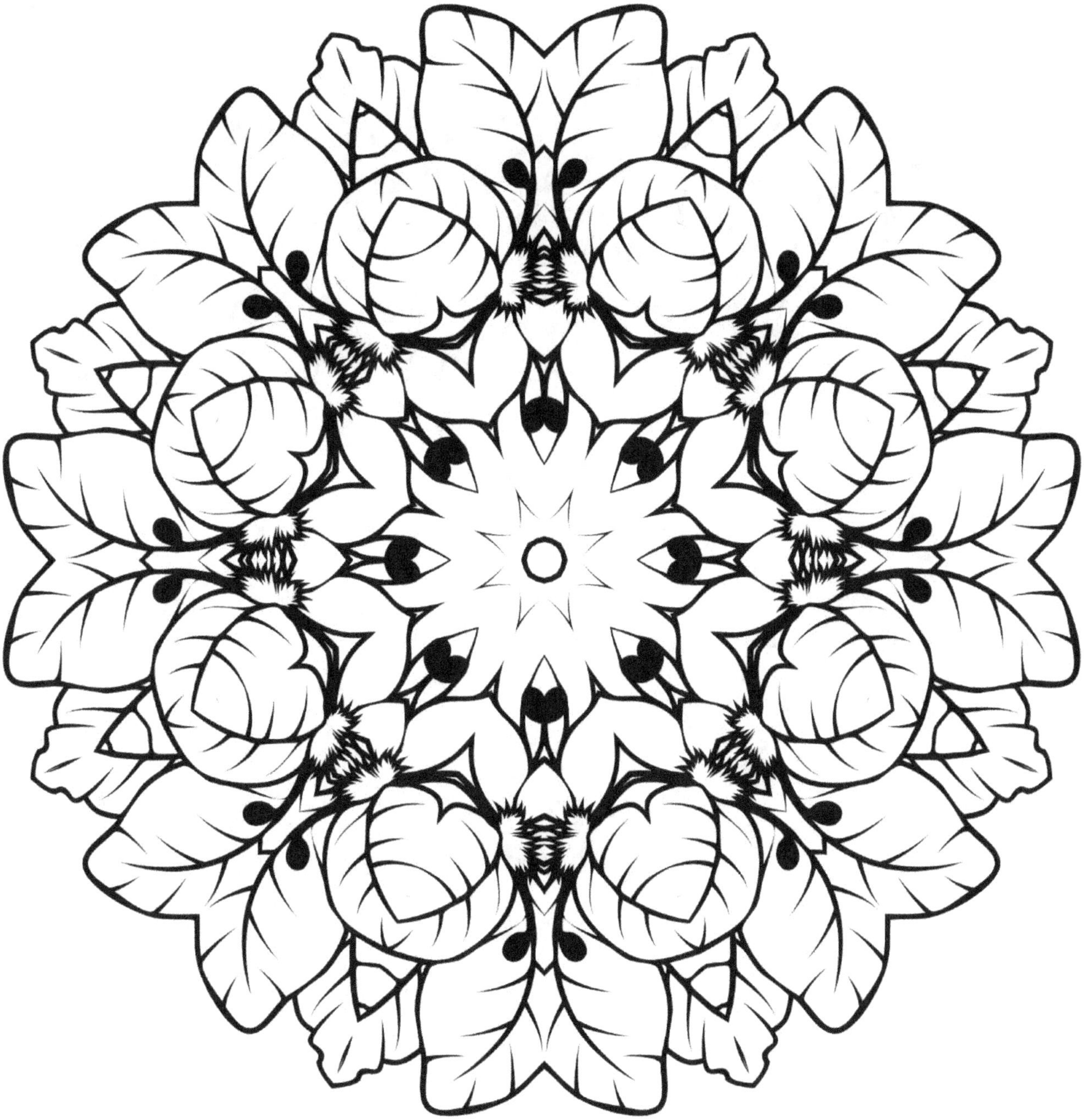

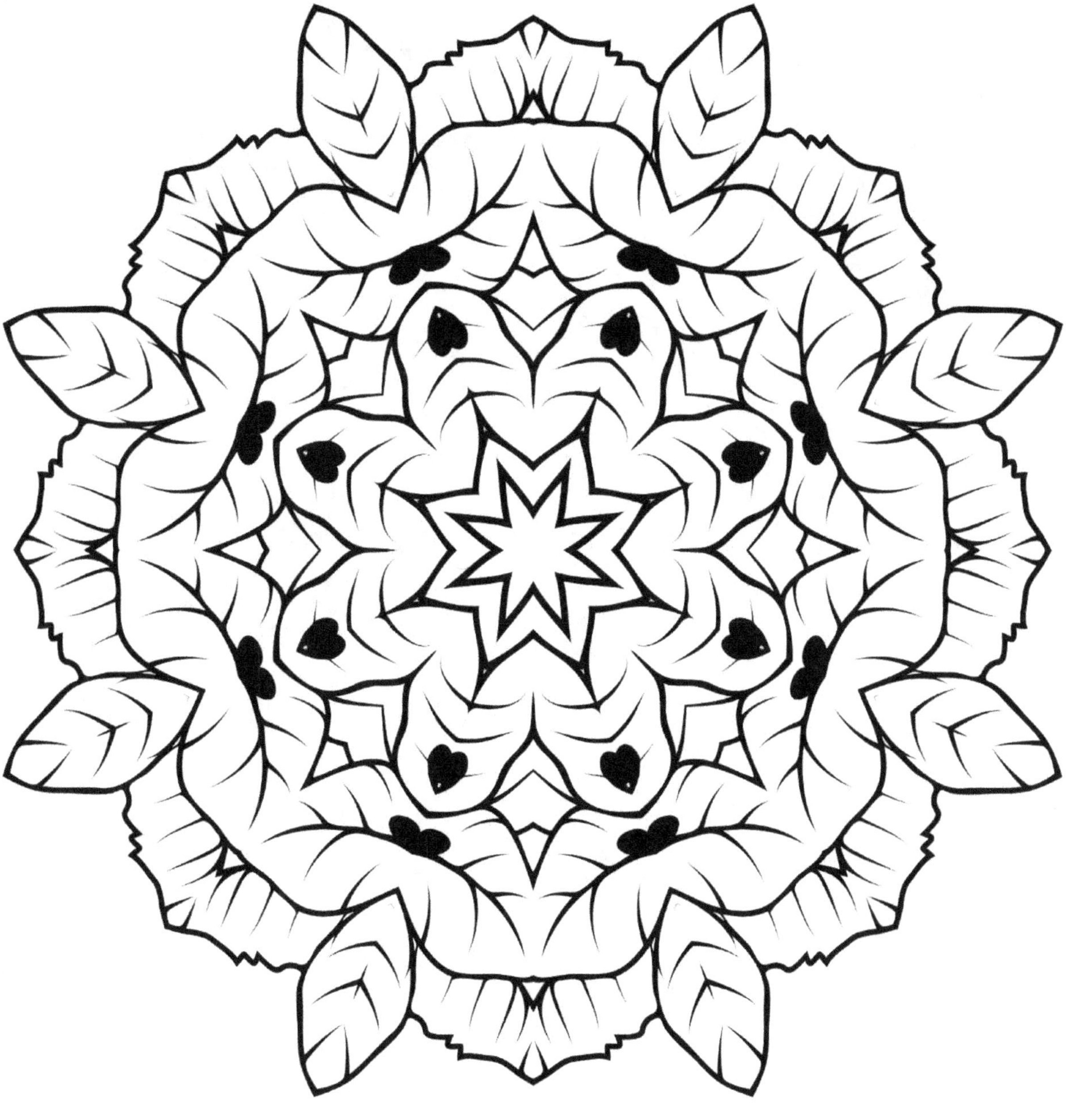

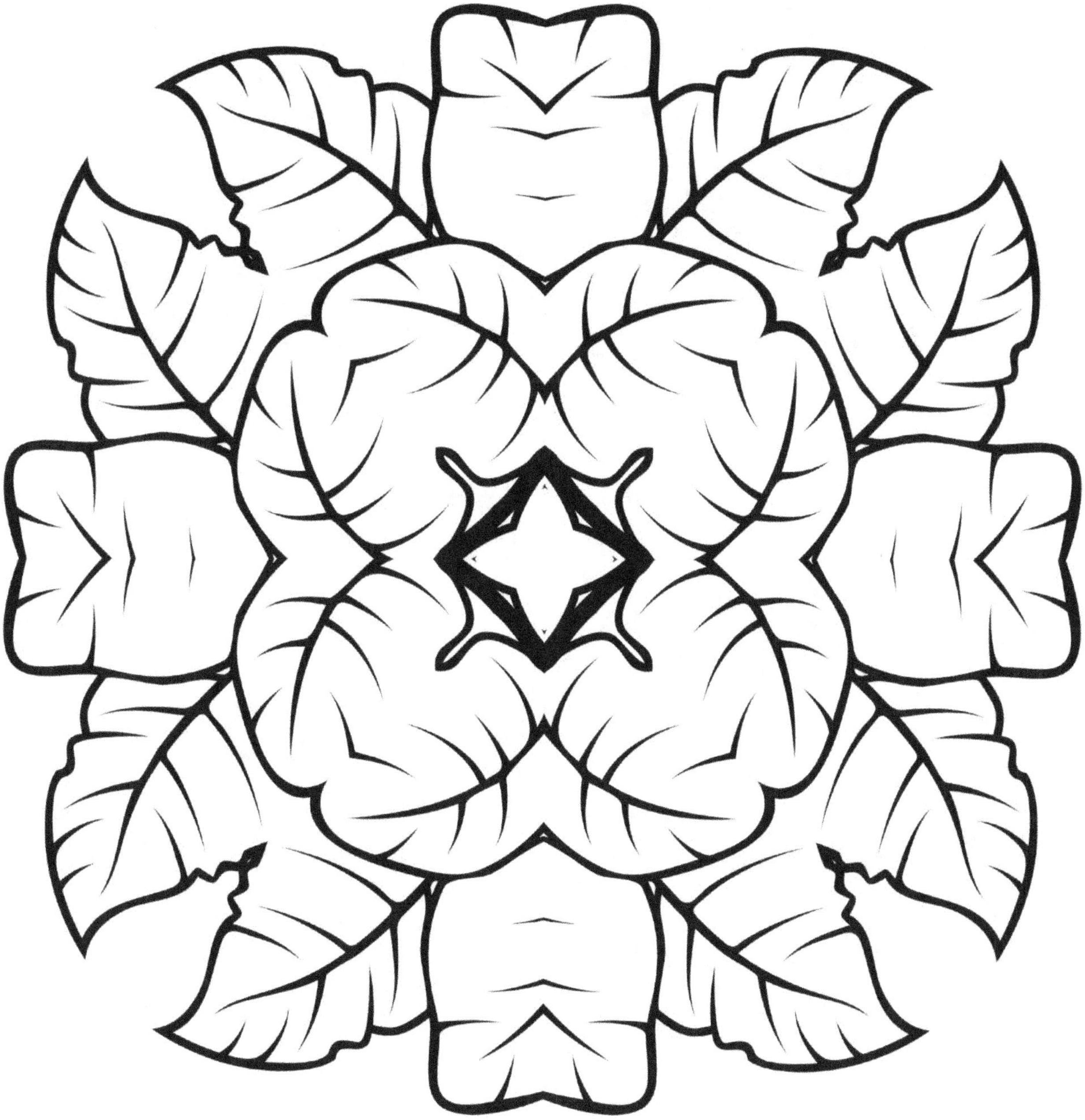

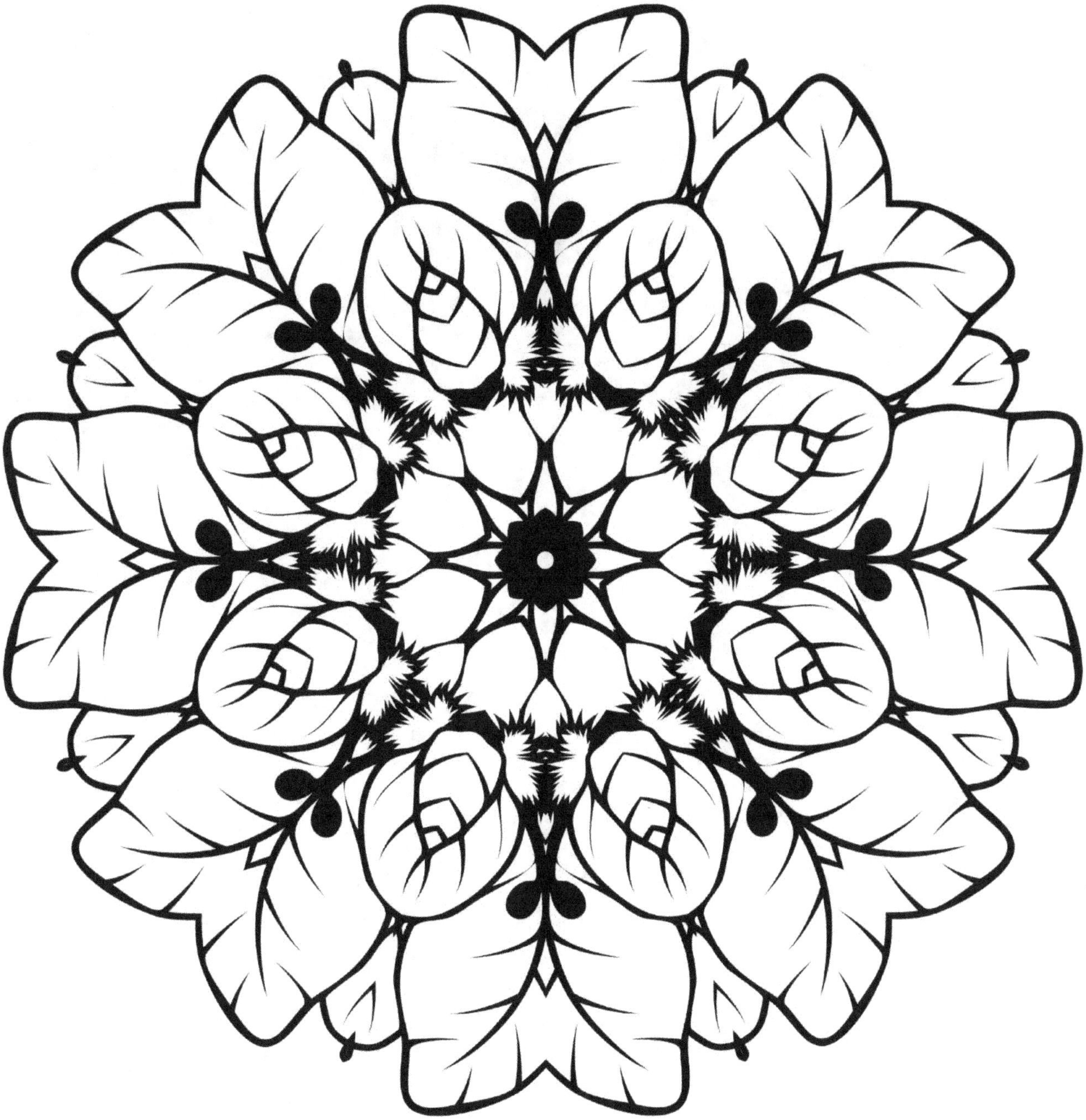

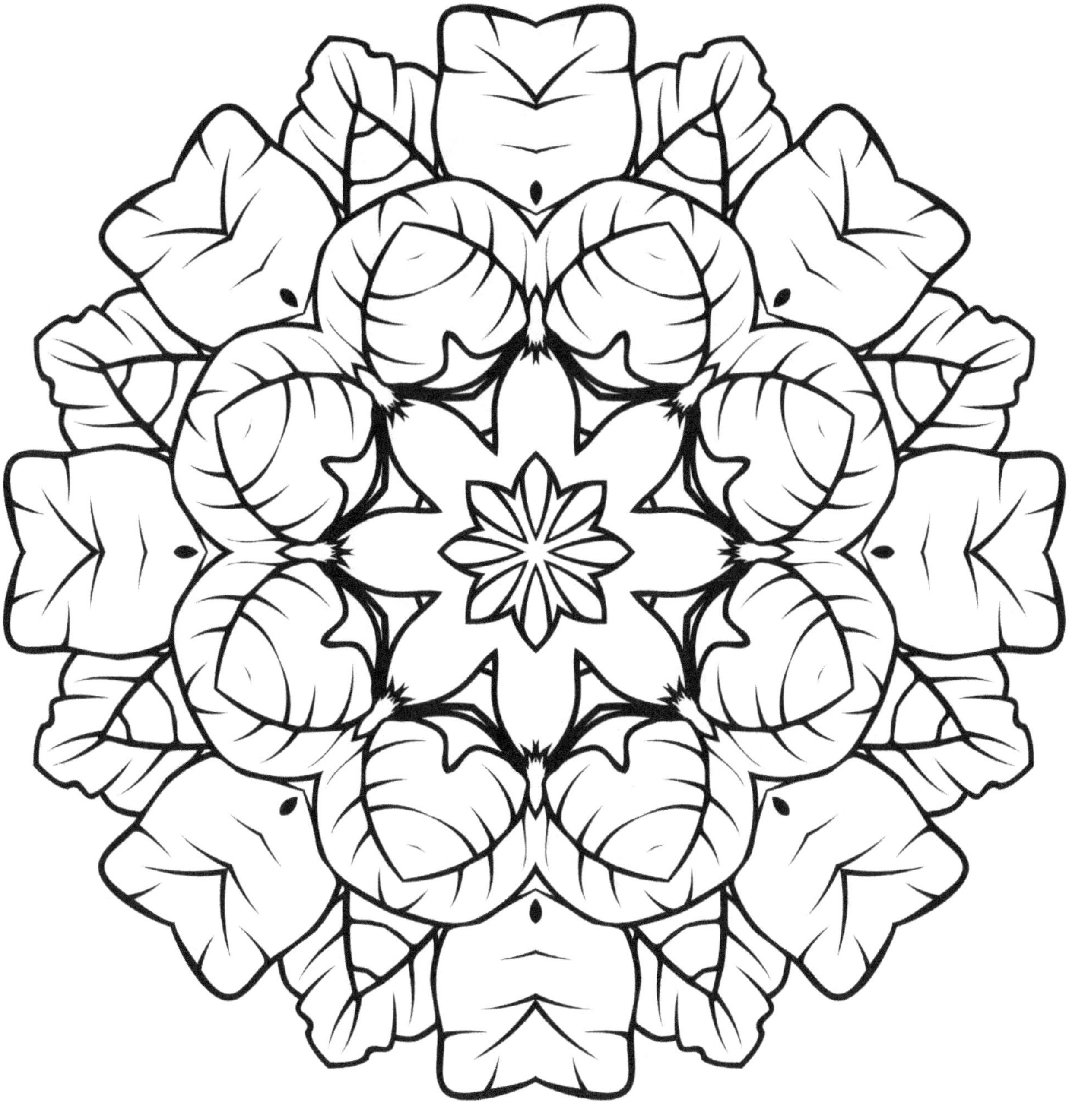

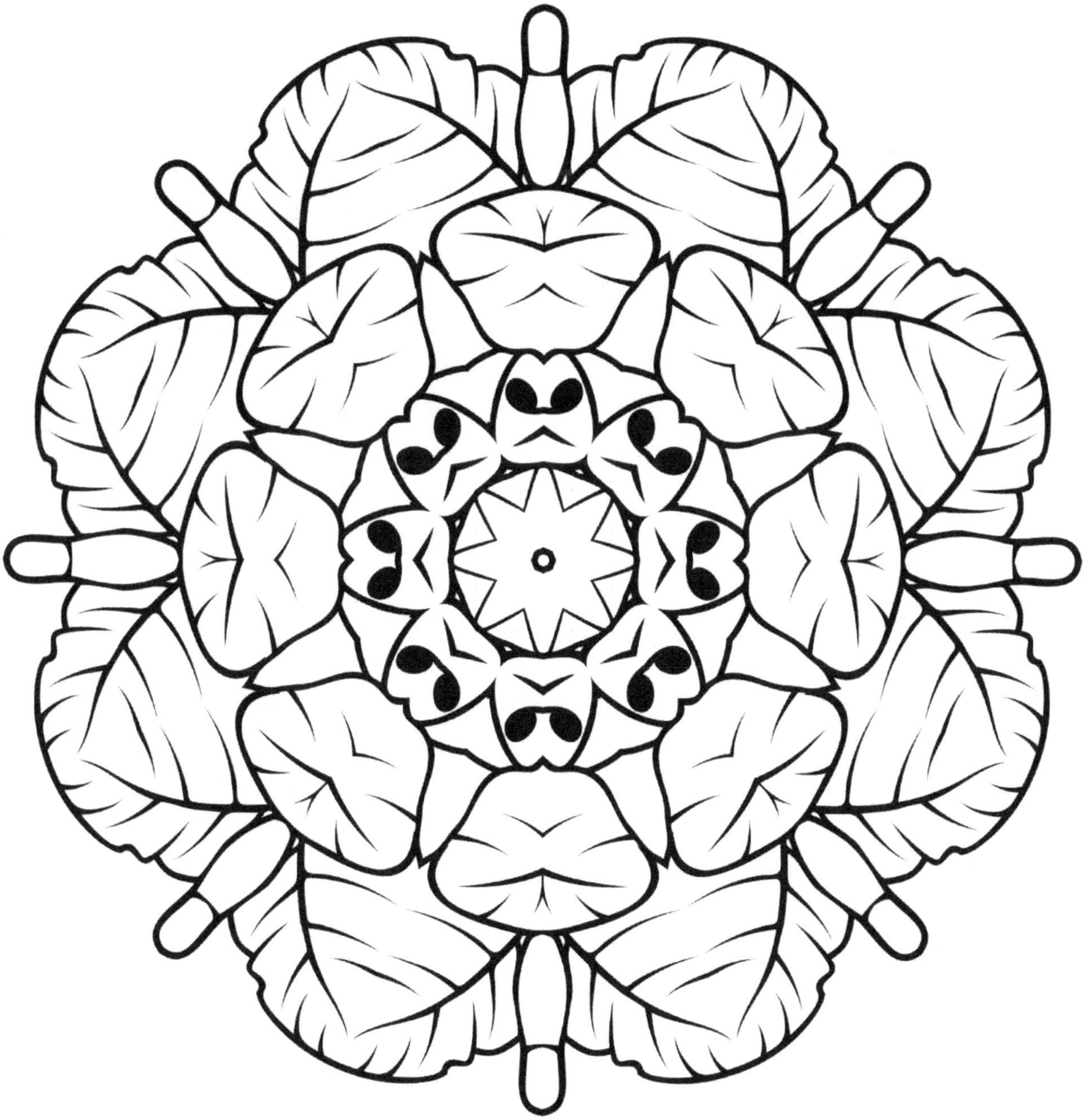

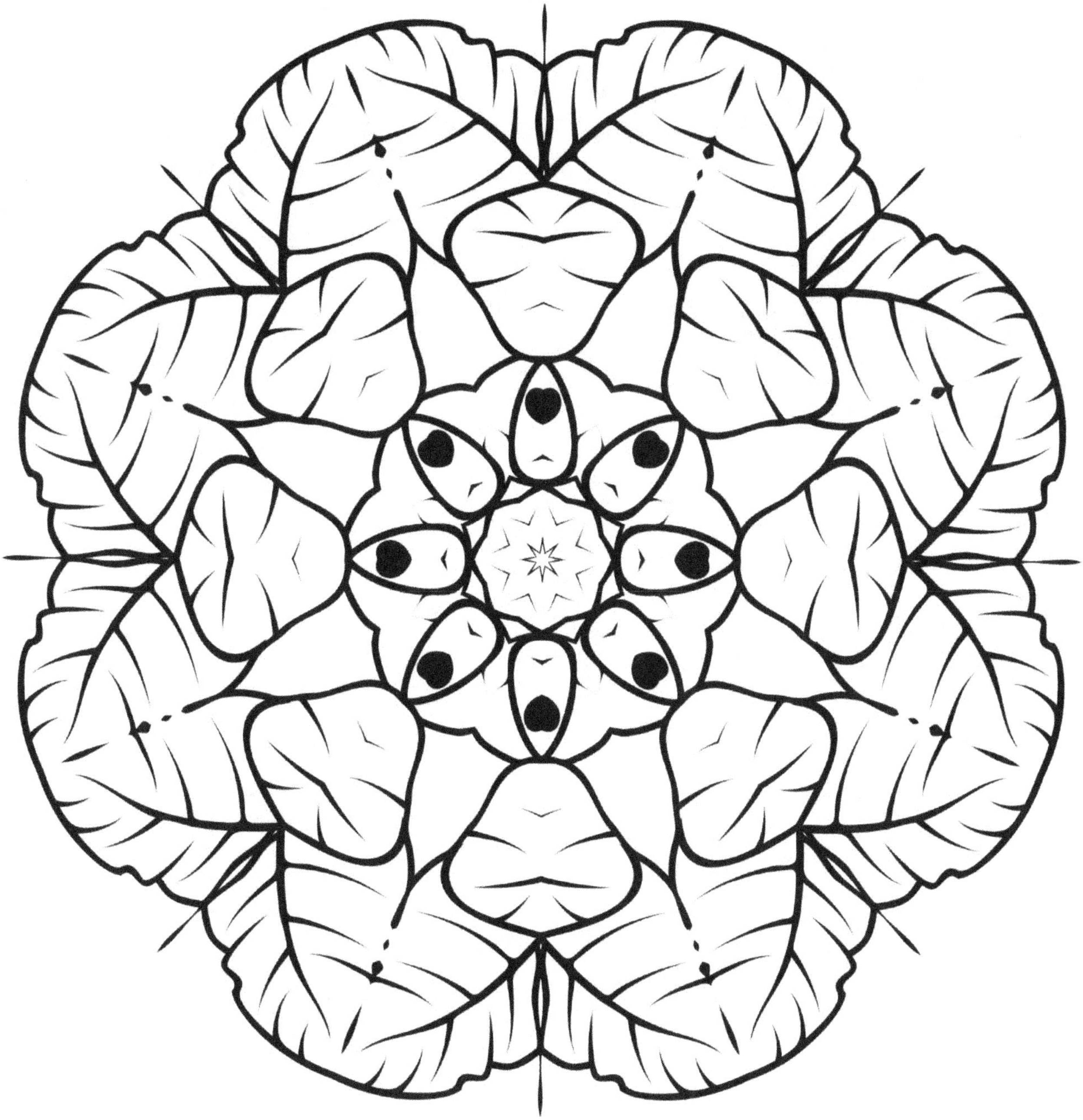

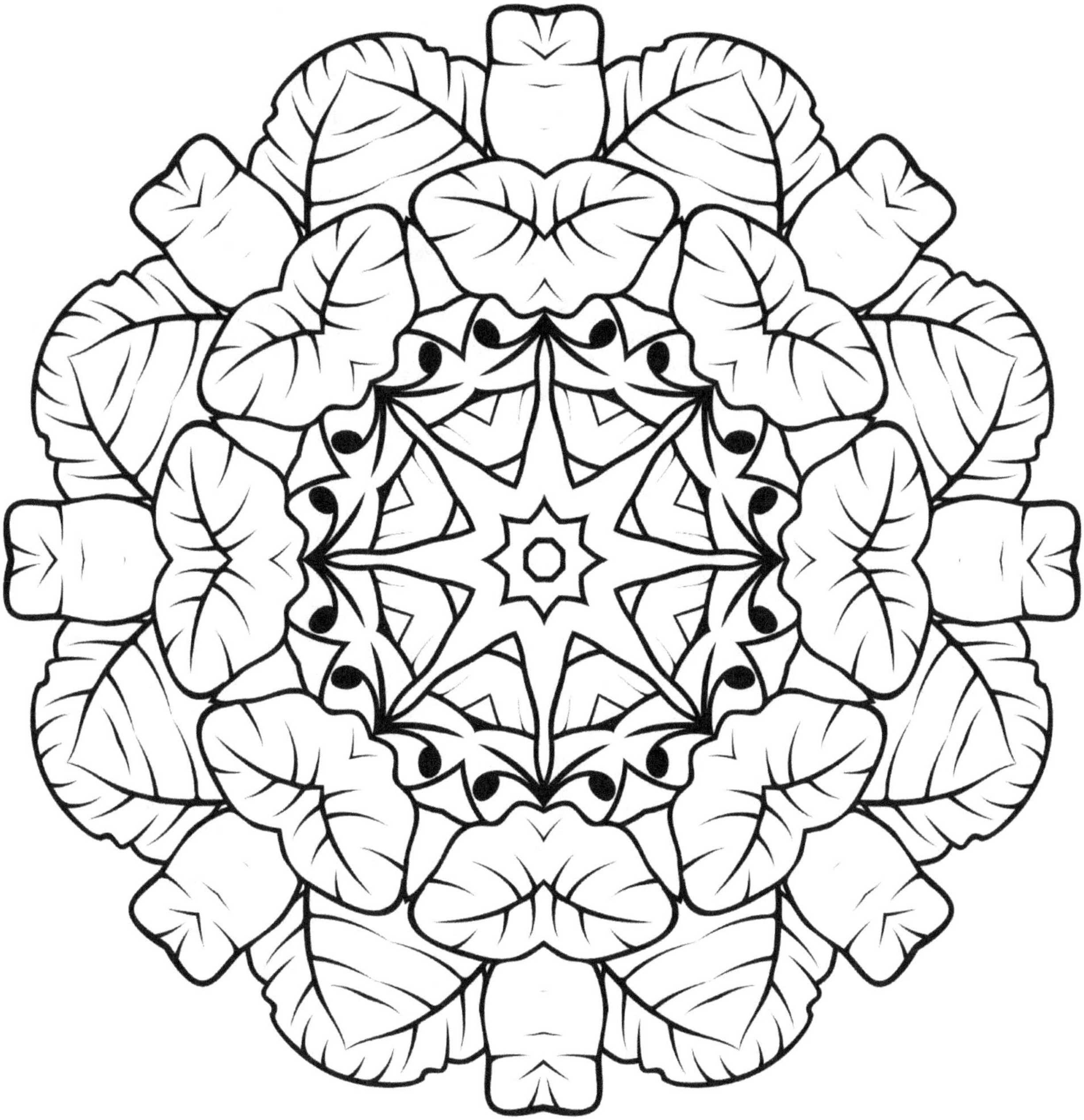

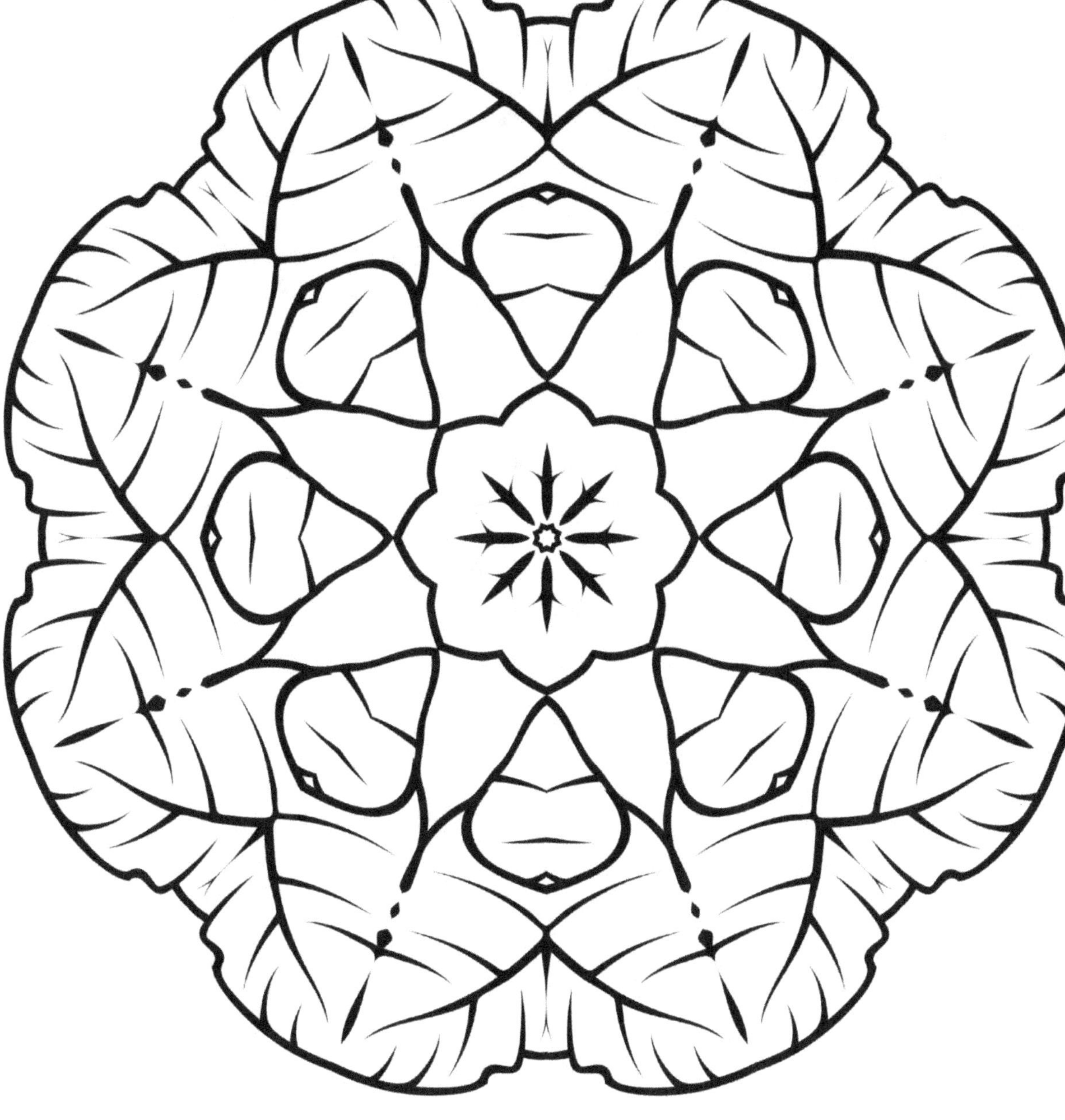

Hope you enjoy this coloring book.

Thank you.

www.ingramcontent.com/pod-product-compliance
Lightning Source LLC
Chambersburg PA
CBHW080833180526
45168CB00006B/2667

* 9 7 8 1 5 1 6 9 5 7 9 0 3 *